NATURE MATTERS

DAVID CONNELL

*To Penny & Tony
from
David Connell*

Transcripts of articles first published in the
Fittleworth and Stopham Village Magazine

All rights reserved. No part of this publication may be reproduced, stored in a retrieval system or transmitted in any form or by any means without the permission of the copyright holder.

Copyright © David Connell

ISBN 978-1-782816-28-7

Introduction

This collection of articles is presented to David Connell in recognition of his extraordinary contribution to our local Magazine over nearly twenty years.

Regular as clockwork, authoritative and informative, and invariably laced with humour, these articles originated when the magazine was primarily a church production and contributions were literally cut, pasted and photocopied to provide the finished product. The articles included here represent just the past seven years' contributions, available in digital form since the magazine became a more general village production.

The Magazine Committee:
Hazel Barkworth
Julie Jillians
Walter Jones
Helen McTeer
Tony Poole
Chris Welfare
Margaret Welfare

The Committee would like to acknowledge the invaluable contribution of two Fittleworth residents: Jules Grammond of G2 Entertainment for looking after the publishing, and Helen McTeer for cover design.

Contents

2009

2	It's spring and the sap is rising	April
4	Butterflies in May	May
6	Buzzards Galore	June
8	Dragonflies - past and present	July
10	Insects on the move	August
12	Natural abilities	September
14	Summer becomes autumn	October
16	Tales of the unexpected	November
18	Why did the chicken cross the road?	December

2010

20	Mid-winter thoughts	January
22	Animals and Snow	February
24	Nature in Art	March
26	Birds in Spring	April
28	In support of microbes	May
30	Amazing rare thoughts	June
32	Unravelling animal behaviour	July
34	A wonderful place for birds	August
36	Summer memories	September
38	A brief look at evolution	October
40	Brownsea Island re-visited	November
42	Wild geese and an elusive butterfly	December

2011

44	Surviving winter	January
46	Fireside Musings	February
48	The first stirrings of spring	March
50	Ants, goldfinches and fossils	April
52	Things we may have missed.	May
54	Collectors become conservationists	June
56	Life in the slow lane.	July
58	The extended family of wasps.	August
60	The quest for purple emperors.	September
62	An enchanted Hampshire Down	October
64	The waterfowl of Petworth Park	November
66	Wildlife along the Arun valley	December

2012

68	Antarctica; a Centenary to remember	January
70	What makes plants grow and birds sing?	February
72	A bird's eye view of Britain	March
74	Where have all the wild flowers gone?	April
76	Spring butterflies	May
78	A spring in two parts & a tragedy remembered	June
80	The charm of sea birds	July
82	What it means to be a bullfinch	August
84	A summer that never was	September
86	Life down a hole	October

88	Birds in disarray	November
90	Do butterflies have built-in sat-nav?	December

2013

92	In praise of cows and waxwings	January
94	2012; the ups and downs of a challenging year	February
96	Birds doing their best in difficult times	March
98	Owls; facts and fantasies	April
100	Life in a pond	May
102	Spring birds and racing snails	June
104	Two squabbles and then briefly summer	July
106	There's more to it than a name	August
108	Grasshoppers & crickets	September
110	Butterflies bounce back	October
112	Epic journeys	November
114	Special times spent amongst birds	December

2014

116	How Important is knowing the name?	January
118	Wildlife and the weather	February
120	More storms and a tale from Mongolia	March
122	Thoughts for April	April
124	Garden birds; winners & losers	May
126	Birds of prey	June
128	The secret lives of robins revealed	July
130	A voyage to Norway and beyond	August
132	The charm of wagtails	September
134	Life as a butterfly	October
136	A new slant on a familiar story	November
138	A look at the year that was	December

2015

140	Our countryside & its wildlife	January
142	Winter musings	February
144	Three birds & a dog called Fred	March
146	Birds in Spring	April
148	From anther to ovule; the pollinators	May
150	A cuckoo's secrets	June
152	The Red Kite's story	July
154	Butterflies may be coping better than we think	August
156	Summer drifts into autumn	September
158	The fascination of nature	October
160	Some good places for birds	November
162	Shades of white - 5 birds and a moth	December

2016

164	The earthworm's salvation	January
166	Now and then	February
168	Survival by adaptation	March

It's spring and the sap is rising

At this time of year nature's attention turns to procreation and the signs are all around us. But sometimes they can be hard to interpret. For example you may see a couple of robins face to face, swaying around with their red breasts all puffed up as if they are a male and female performing a sort of square dance. But in reality they are a both males saying "Look mate, this is my patch. And anyway, my chest is bigger and redder than yours so clear off." Male blackbirds, their beaks now bright orange, seem for ever to be chasing each other around under the bushes with the same message, whilst other song birds are content with the more peaceful tactic of serenading their mates with a song which also warns off rivals.

Once paired birds split up the marital duties in a variety of ways. Often males take part in both nest-building and incubation as well as feeding the young. But in the case of, say, a kestrel the male plays no part in the incubation but instead is in sole charge of feeding both his mate on the nest and, in due course, the young. When food is short this task can be so arduous that he may loose as much as a third of his body-weight. If this sounds tough consider the lot of a male red-necked phalarope. This pretty little bird, much like a moorhen in size and behaviour, seldom comes to this country but breeds in the tundra. All the female does is lay eggs in a shallow hollow on bare ground. Thereafter everything - incubation, feeding the young, the lot - is left to the male. So extreme is this role-reversal that the male has even adopted the more sombre plumage which typically provides females with protective camouflage when on the nest. It must give little joy to these ill-used fathers to know that there are other bird-species wherein the males, having settled their mates down on eggs, are secretly polygamous.

Another sign of spring is the croaking of frogs recently returned to their natal breeding ponds. Some of the more ardent males will have set up quarters there the previous autumn in order to be on the spot when the females arrive some time the following March. Since they traded in their gills for lungs when they stopped being tadpoles, this strategy obliges them to subsist all winter on what little oxygen they can absorb from the water through their skins and therefore runs the risk that should the pond freeze over and toxic gases get trapped beneath the ice they will perish.

Moles are unlikely to occupy our thoughts unless they happen to throw up mounds in our garden. Nonetheless there are interesting things going on underground. A mole will not normally tolerate the presence of another in its network of burrows so a male must first find a way of detecting the whereabouts of a prospective mate in a neighbouring burrow, then tunnel his way in, pay his respects and then hot-foot it back home as quick as he can before getting bitten.

In the case of the larger mammals the males are bigger and stronger than females. This serves the triple purpose of equipping them to fight for a mate, hunt for food and defend their families. But sometimes the male embellishment serves only for fighting. For example each year stags grow massive antlers which they use solely to ward off any other male which attempts to steal one of their harem. They have no other purpose and can inflict terrible wounds on an opponent. Male adders, on the other hand, are smaller than females which have to carry eggs and then give birth to live babies. In spring the males fight each other by rearing up and coiling their upper bodies round each other. The object is to wrestle your opponent to the ground. But fangs are never used and great care is taken to inflict no serious harm. The loser simply slinks away in shame but is still free and able to try his luck again another time.

April 2009

Butterflies in May

A long time ago I was at a school where the cricket master was a kindly old gentleman much the same shape as a pear. He also taught French so what more natural than that we 9 & 10 year-olds, when out of ear-shot, should call him La Poire! Thus it was that early one May I found myself amongst a gathering of other small boys at the edge of the playing field to receive instruction from Monsieur la Poire on the correct position of feet, head and wrists necessary to secure the perfect cover-drive. After a while, as I remember it, discipline would crumble and this enabled me to turn my attention to the butterflies in the nearby rough grass and it was on one such occasion that I saw my first ever orange tip.

Ever since those days this little butterfly has been, for me, the quintessence of spring. It is usually out and about in time to add lustre to the scene for our annual Village Garden Trail and in fact this year I saw the first one on the extremely early date of April 6th. Another favourite butterfly on the wing early in May is the holly blue. Identification is easy because there are no other blue butterflies about so early in the year. The males hatch a few days before the females and this allows time for them to check out the lie of the land and find unhatched chrysalises which they then perch beside in anticipation of a potential mate emerging. I have even read somewhere that male holly blues can tell the gender of the chrysalis before it hatches which, if true, saves them from a lot of unnecessary hanging around.

In addition to garden butterflies there are a couple of national rarities to be seen towards the end of May in places which are not too far from here and which are well worth a visit in their own right. The first is Oaken Woods just north of Shillinglee where conservationists keep conditions just right for wood whites. These are dainty little butterflies wherein the male courts his lady in a manner which is unique amongst lepidoptera; he stands an inch in front of her and extends his proboscis, normally used only for feeding, which he then waves around as if conducting an orchestra, an odd antic which seems to enchant her. And if you fail to see this performance you will be consoled by the local bird-song which may include nightingales and maybe also by finding butterfly orchids in the long grass along the edges of the rides.

And the other needs a trip to the Isle of Wight where, on the downs above Niton there are Glanville fritillaries to be found amongst a carpets of wild flowers. This is the only place in this country where you can see them although across the Channel they are not that rare. They are named after the famous 17th century entomologist Lady Eleanor Glanville whose will, you may remember, was disputed by disgruntled relatives who sought to have it set aside under the Acts of Lunacy on the grounds that anyone who spent as much time as her Ladyship in pursuit of butterflies must be of unsound mind. The courts were not persuaded but even so the matter is unsettling to the author of these notes who, in the view of some, is similarly smitten.

And finally comes more news which confirms that our climate is changing the rhythms of nature; this time a call from Little Bognor to say that the first swallows had just returned to their usual nest in a garage. The date was 8th April which beats by eight days last year, itself an all-time record for this particular place. And, as I sign off, we down here on the south side of the village have just heard our first cuckoo. So there!!

May 2009

Nature Matters

Buzzards Galore

In the course of chatting to a visitor who came to our recent Garden Trail he told me that, as a glider pilot, he had often seen our village from the air but never before had he explored it at ground level. He had not, he said, realised what a nice place Fittleworth is, nor what pretty gardens we have. I, on the other hand, was more interested to hear whether it was true that glider pilots often use buzzards to locate favourable air currents. He said that as a rule they - the pilots - knew for themselves where to go but on a still day if they saw buzzards soaring around, pilots would know that the birds were on to a good thing and join them. But what was really interesting about what he said was that sometimes the reverse happens; buzzards use the gliders to seek out the best places. To illustrate the point our visitor told me that recently he had had no less than five buzzards so close to his wingtips that he feared a collision, especially when the birds started to perform their aerial display which involves elaborate twists and tumbles and the clasping of each others talons. One day recently, he said, he had also been joined by a red kite.

Given the number of buzzards around here these days it's hard to remember that only ten years ago you had to go as far west as Dorset or Wiltshire to see one. Oddly enough, despite their size and prowess as hunters they are slow to spread into new territory, even where there is abundant food and plenty of nesting sites. This is confirmed by work done in the west country which revealed that when breeding concentration in an established area reaches an unsustainable density, the birds will reduce the number of eggs they lay rather than disburse. This is odd but none-the-less explains why their recent spread into Sussex from the west is still mostly confined to this end of the county.

The birds which we have moved in here are sometimes called common buzzards which distinguishes them from two other buzzard species on the British list. One is the honey buzzard which passes through as a passage migrant in spring and autumn, sometimes in considerable numbers. They feed on the bees and wasps from which, using their huge beaks, they remove the sting before swallowing. And finally, just to keep the twitchers on their toes, there are rough- legged buzzards, rare winter visitors along the east coast and distinguished, as their name suggests, by having feathers on their legs all the way down to their feet.

Buzzards take a couple of years to attain full adult plumage and even then can be very variable in shade of colour. But around here there is little else to confuse them with, except perhaps a red kite which has a deeply-forked tail and slow, lazy flight. Up in Scotland buzzards have the knick-name "the tourist's eagle". This is because so many visitors who are eager to see a golden eagle spot the much more common, smaller buzzard and send postcards home telling everyone that they have seen the iconic eagle.

June 2009

Dragonflies - past and present

Three hundred million years ago a form of insect which had recently risen from beneath the water, was flying around over marshy swamps that would one day become our coal-fields. It had a wing-span of about 30 inches but in other respects was much like the dragonflies which we know to-day. Never-the-less it is almost certain that these huge insects failed to survive subsequent changes in the earth's atmosphere and that we must wait a further half a million years for the true ancestors of our present-day dragonflies to appear. Evidence from fossils tells us that these later insects bore such a close resemblance to what we know to-day that it is even possible to relate them to individual families. In other words dragonflies seem to have met and survived without difficulty all the immense environmental changes of the past 2.5 million. This is extraordinary, as can be seen when compared with the progress, in evolutionary terms, made by our own ancestors. Early man had not even appeared 2.5 million years ago, so let us pick up the story much more recently, say half a million years ago by which time our ancestors had just learnt to make a fire. Since then progress by their successors (us) has been rapid; we have for example developed the skills to build the Great Wall of China, paint the Sistine Chapel, put a man on the moon and construct the internet. Dragonflies, meanwhile, have been content with their ability to hover, fly backwards, side-ways and forwards and see in all directions at the same time.

So what, exactly, do we have to-day? Well, for the purposes of classification the order "dragonflies" (odonata) is divided into two sub-orders; true dragonflies and damselflies. These are easy to tell apart; dragonflies are large, very fast and direct in flight and have huge eyes which meet over the front of their heads. When they settle their wings are held out to the side like an airplane. All this makes them rather scary but in reality they don't bite, sting or do anything nasty except to other insects which they catch and eat. By comparison damselflies are small, flit daintily through water-side vegetation, fold their wings back along their bodies when settled and have eyes which, though large, are far less bulbous than dragonflies. Both have transparent wings which glitter in the sun and brightly-coloured bodies. All in all these blameless insects add lustre to the summer scene and it is perhaps to their advantage that their beautiful colours fade quickly when they die, thus saving them from the attention of collectors who might otherwise decimate their numbers for display in a cabinet.

Despite their robust appearance an adult dragonfly will be lucky to live much longer than three weeks. It's purpose is purely to mate and paired couples can often be seen flying in tandem, the male holding the female by the scruff of her neck in claspers situated at the end of his body. This may be either a prelude to mating or, especially in the case of damselflies, a post-mating procedure whereby the male leads his partner off to lay eggs. This she does either by dipping her ovipositor beneath the surface of the water and attaching the egg to vegetation or skimming along the top so that the eggs wash off and sink. Some hatch in about a month, others the following spring. The resulting nymphs move on legs and feed on other small inhabitants of the pond. Like all animals that have inelastic skins they must moult to allow their bodies to grow. This happens about eight times after which they climb up out of the water using a reed-stem, split open their skins and out steps an adult dragonfly. It takes a further half an hour for the wings to expand and a couple of days for the body-colours to reach their full glory. But these often change and fade as the insect ages and elderly females can assume the colour of a male; all very confusing and identification is a nightmare. But knowing their names is not an essential part of enjoying their beauty.

July 2009

Insects on the move

Painted ladies are not only strikingly beautiful butterflies but are also possessed of three characteristics not usually found together in the same species. First, they are very strong flyers; second, they have a questing spirit and third, given favourable conditions, they can complete a full life-cycle from egg to adult in about a month. At no stage do they need to hibernate. As a result they can spread themselves over vast distances in the space of one season, limited only by the inability of their caterpillars to survive in temperatures below 5°c. The painted ladies we get here come from North Africa having started their journey by the end of February. They fly north breeding as they go, so that the migration is more the result of a relay by successive generations than a marathon by individuals.

Numbers reaching this country therefore depend on conditions both in North Africa and en route and if both are favourable we here can be inundated by migrants. This last happened in 1997 and seemed all set to happen again this year after heavy winter rains in the Atlas mountains produced inordinate amounts of thistles for the caterpillars to feed on. The first wave of butterflies to reach this country was in late May when the papers reported that 3000 were counted coming in over Portland Bill in just one hour. How such a precise number was counted we are not told but what I can say is that when we were on the Isle of Wight a couple weeks later and visited the south coast between Seaview and Ventnor the headlands were seething with new arrivals desperate to feed up on any flower they could find. But then, after the initial onslaught things seem to have quietened down so that the few that are around as I write these notes a month later are obviously home-bred; very fresh-looking with none of the wear and tear which suggests a long journey. So maybe breeding conditions across the continent have not been good enough to maintain the early momentum. No doubt the next few weeks will tell.

For another story relating to the unusual movement of insects we are indebted to Mr Charles Moore, one-time editor of the Daily Telegraph and now a columnist with the Spectator. Mr Moore lives in Sussex with his wife who is Nature Correspondent for their local village magazine. It transpires that Mrs Moore has a moth trap, a device which uses a lamp to attract and hold moths long enough for them to be identified and then released unharmed back into the wild, and that a recent night's haul included a Rannoch looper. This little moth is, as its name suggests, normally found only in Scotland and this was its first recorded appearance in Sussex, an event all the more startling as such things are usually attributed to climate change with movements from south to north rather than the reverse. Mr and Mrs Moore are especially elated by their visitor as it has laid some eggs in their garden and promises to establish a small colony. Their wish to offer succour to the visitors here in Sussex is all the greater since there is the chance that they have come to settle, not from elsewhere in Britain but from the Continent, thus providing them with the opportunity to defy the aims of the B.N.P.

August 2009

Natural abilities

Albert Trott (Albertrott to his mates) is an excellent example of a man possessed of almost superhuman abilities. In his case they related to eyesight, speed of reflex and brute strength. Born in Australia, he played cricket for then three of the Ashes Tests in 1894/95, after which he was dropped. He came here and in 1899 was included in the MCC side which played his former team-mates at Lords. He proceeded to hit their best bowler twice into the pavilion for six and then, just for good measure, struck him straight over the pavilion and out of the ground, the ball finally bouncing off a neighbouring chimney. No batsman since has succeeded in clearing the pavilion at Lords. Over the next few years Trott continued to demonstrate his prodigious talents around the world until, at the age of 41, he committed suicide. There is however another Trott, Jonathon, now in the frame to play for England. The ancestry is not confirmed but maybe just maybe...who know!!.

There are, of course, other examples of people with exceptional gifts but by and large we humans usually stand in awe of the abilities possessed by other life-forms and the truth is that we owe our position at the top of the tree of life to the possession of a brain far superior to those of other living things. This, in conjunction with nimble fingers, gives us the ability to invent tools which we use to do what other life-forms can do unaided. For example most of us would be pushed to see a match-stick with a naked eye more than 20 feet away so we invent binoculars and telescopes. Even then we cannot match a bird of prey; to do so we would need eyes the size of a grapefruit. And consider the bats which hunt at night; they catch air-borne prey by making little squeaking sounds which bounce back and are picked up by nerves in their wings. The bat then swoops in and catches its meal. We say how clever and invent radar. Then there are moths, another night-flyer. They rely on a sense of smell and have developed extraordinarily efficient antennae which enable them to filter out all other smells and locate the whereabouts of a prospective mate, sometimes at a range of four or five hundreds yards. If we have a need for such a device I suppose the French provide it by offering small, expensive bottles containing an essence with the word Perfume on the label. Or perhaps even better we can now buy pocket-sized devices which enable us to broadcast our message world-wide in an instant.

An albatross can leave its fluffy white chick the size of a football alone on the snow-covered ground whilst it covers several hundred miles of Antarctic waste in search of food and can still come back to precisely the same spot where she left her chick, maybe days before. We have navigational aids but I doubt anything as good as that.

Now for something different; the second half of the summer has seen an explosion of butterflies. The painted ladies which dominated last month's notes have had a second wind and have been joined by an influx of large whites from across the Channel to augment our native population. Commas and red admirals have been allover our flowers and up on the Downs are reports of 3,000 chalkhill blues just on one stretch of down land alone. Even here we were visited briefly by a white admiral and silver-washed fritillary, both plentiful this year in places like Ebernoe Common but never before on the brambles behind our compost heap. There has been much else besides to warm the heart but two butterflies in particular are worth a mention; peacocks and small tortoiseshells. The increasing scarcity of both in the past few years was causing alarm and their re-appearance in such numbers is therefore all the more welcome. Both will spend the winter as adults; survivors will breed again next spring. Both come into houses to hibernate and are at risk if, after going to sleep, indoor heating wakes them up. So if you have such a visitor the kindest thing is to re-locate it to a sheltered but unheated place where it can pass the winter undisturbed.

September 2009

Nature Matters

Summer becomes autumn

There comes a moment when you can sense that the business of summer is done. This year, for some, that may have been when, one Sunday afternoon late in August after several weeks of national anxiety, we finally won back the Ashes. And that, for the time being, was that. For others it may be enough to sniff the air and observe the countryside. Birds which came here just for the summer have departed and those which live here permanently are skulking around in the bushes soundless and moulting. The few butterflies still to be seen are tatty and on their last legs and everywhere the vegetation consists of little more than the odd empty seed-head poking up through dank grass. Even the occasional warm day fails to lighten the mood of fading glory.

And so to autumn, a time of crisp morning air, bright blue skies and a countryside lit up by trees which are turning every colour from yellow to shades of gold and bronze. Birds reappear in their smart new winter plumage which will see them through until after next year's breeding is done, whilst others arrive from the north, driven here by harsh weather and need to find food. Redwings, members of the thrush family from Scandinavia, appear wherever there are berries to eat and have usually stripped the holly trees by the time we need them for Christmas. Its the same with the larger fieldfares although these are equally at home eating insects on newly ploughed land.

Other visitors which are less easy to spot are those which are the same species as our own native birds; finches, tits, pigeons and suchlike. These incomers may be just passing through en route to places like Spain but any that stay will certainly have departed for home by next spring so they never inter-breed with our own residents. For this reason they develop small characteristics either in plumage, behaviour or call-note which remain unique to themselves. Usually it takes an expert to spot these differences but sometimes if you see the two alongside each other on the bird-table it might just be possible. In the butterfly world I used to notice this same thing when we took our holidays down in southern France, driving down in easy stages with frequent stops on the way just to stretch the legs or whatever. In those days heath fritillaries were well-distributed along the way but always in self-contained colonies with very little movement between each. As a result it was easy to spot small variations in wing-markings as we proceeded on our journey, none sufficiently significant to qualify as a distinct new species in its own right (that would mean that they were incapable of inter-breeding) but none-the less discernable.

One of the special joys of living in these parts is that we are so well placed to see the huge influx of wildfowl and wetland birds that come to this country each winter. Anywhere from the Wiggonholt Reserve along the Arun Valley and anywhere around Chichester harbour and Pagham are rich hunting grounds for waterfowl. Numbers build up from October onwards and reach a peak in December, January and February. At Wiggonholt a special joy is the huge flocks of wigeon and lapwing interspersed with pintail, teal, shoveller and gadwell. Wigeon spend much of the day grazing in waterside meadows and, if alarmed by say a passing peregrine falcon, they rise up, maybe several hundred in a single flock, and wheel around in circles making a very distinctive whistling sound. To be there and witness such an event late in the day just as the sun is setting behind the Downs is to experience birding at its very best.

October 2009

Tales of the unexpected

So off, then, for a week in the west country. First stop was a B & B near Wareham where fellow-guests recommended a visit to Brownsea Island in Poole Harbour. This is a place well-known for its wildlife but I must admit that I have always wondered how an island which is in the middle of so much maritime activity, overlooked by real estate ranked as amongst the most expensive in the country, and heavily promoted by the local Tourist Board could possibly be the right setting in which to enjoy the company of wild animals.

But I need not have worried; the National Trust own the island and the part which is of greatest interest to a naturalist is managed with quiet efficiency by The Dorset Wildlife Trust. The main feature is a non-tidal lagoon composed of mudflats, saltings and shallow brackish water. Small islands provide nesting sites for terns and two well-placed hides allow visitors to get close to the birds without disturbing them. Our visit in the first week in September was too early to catch the full force of winter migrants but it was enough that greenshank, fresh in from Scandinavia, teal, close enough to see their emerald-green wing feathers with the naked eye along with other little gems were all feeding just beside the hides. A little further off was a mixed flock of black-tailed godwits and avocets. And then the day's star turn; eight spoonbills. These huge white birds, the size of a heron with massive spatulate bills, seldom come to this country and when they do, always cause a stir. So one way and another we had a memorable day. Plus, since you ask, we did catch a fleeting glimpse of the island's iconic red squirrels and Bridget has a photograph to prove it.

Next stop was Bigbury in South Devon to stay with friends who have a house right on the edge of the cliff overlooking the bay; an idyllic setting from which to witness an event which was as spectacular as it was unexpected. This is what happened; early one morning I heard the unmistakable call of raptors and there, twenty yards from our bedroom window, was a very agitated peregrine falcon circling above the cliff. Coming from the other direction were a pair of buzzards. Now a peregrine has the reputation for being, pound-for-pound, the most efficient killing machine in the animal world. But a buzzard is a third bigger and a useful fighter in its own right. So I was amazed to see the peregrine fold its wings and stoop at the buzzards which immediately dropped down out of sight below the cliff. A couple of seconds later, the peregrine and one of the buzzards reappeared fleetingly, talons interlocked as they grappled in mid-air. Then they were gone. I never saw the buzzards again but shortly afterwards the insouciance with which the peregrine flew back across the scene of battle left no doubt who had come off best. Amazingly I have since read that buzzards feature as regular items on a peregrine's menu along with harriers and ravens.

A couple of other bits of news come from the Sussex Wildlife Trust magazine. The first tells us that, this spring, a robin was found to have taken over a blackbird's nest and laid five eggs in it and the second concerns butterflies which were in the pupal stage during the cold snap of last June, a number of which hatched into adults which were unusually dark. White admirals, purple emperors and silver-washed fritillaries in particular were affected. Such aberrations were much prized in former times by collectors, but breeders then started to produce them artificially and in so doing wrecked the market.

And finally a report from Little Bognor where Janet Hester was surprised to see a flock of racing pigeons come in and, like duck, land directly onto her mill-pond, spreading out their wings as if to cool down and have a drink. Once refreshed, they took off again straight from the water. I have read that wood pigeons have been known to do this but it is quite something to see for oneself.

November 2009

Why did the chicken cross the road?

This is a question which has fascinated man since time immemorial. Roman fishermen knew exactly when to expect the arrival of tuna each spring. What they probably did not know was that these fish were following and hunting herrings as they moved from the cold waters of the Atlantic into the warmth of the Mediterranean to spawn. All this illustrates nicely the two main reasons for relocation in the animal world; either to find suitable places to breed (in this case the herrings) or in pursuit of food (the tuna). Other animal movements have exercised some of the great thinkers of the day down the ages and some odd conclusions were drawn. Thus 3000 years ago the Greek philosopher Aristotle wrote that redstarts disappeared in winter because they turned into robins. And in 1186 the state of ignorance was still such that when a Welsh clergyman went to Ireland and said that he had seen with his own eyes shells hanging in threads from floating timber which, as they grew, turned into geese. This was accepted wisdom for the next 500 years and indeed the myth lives on to this day in the name given to the barnacle geese which come here from arctic Russia each winter.

As recently as the late 1700s no less a naturalist than Gilbert White was saying that swallows hibernate in riverbank burrows and it was left to Harry Witherby, publisher of *British Birds Journal* and later co-author of *The Handbook Of British Birds* who, in 1909 wrote an article in his Journal asking his readers to join him in a programme of bird-ringing which would uncover the secrets of bird migration. From this small beginning we now know as much about the movement of birds as we do about anything else in the natural world.

Bird migration certainly catches the imagination of the casual naturalist but consider also the salmon, born from eggs laid in fresh-water rivers by parents which have swum against strong currents and leapt up waterfalls to reach their destination. The young salmon then spend anything from one to four years before swimming down-stream and out perhaps a thousand miles into the open sea. After about 4 years they return to their natal river, swim on up-stream, lay eggs in precisely the same place where they themselves were born and then, very possibly, die. How they navigate is still a bit of a mystery but the real achievement is to have developed gills and kidneys which enable them to move from fresh to salt water with such ease. Eels can do the same but the other way round. They live and feed in fresh water but go far out to sea to breed.

Then there are lemmings, small rodents native to Scandinavia. What gets them moving is an explosion in population and the consequent need to disperse. This happens every 4 or 5 years when the number of litters per pair doubles and the average litter increases from 4 to 6. There is no obvious trigger for this but the extraordinary thing is that other unrelated animals which share the same habitat have the same cycle of increased fertility. Thus "lemming years" are also years for huge numbers of shrews, capercaillies and certain butterflies. Another odd thing about lemmings is that they always move north and even when they reach fresh areas with abundant food they still press on blindly as if in search of something which they never find. And if a cliff intervenes they happily fall over it to their death. This has made poor lemmings a metaphor for stupidity.

Other examples of dispersal are provided by insects such as bees, termites and the migratory locusts which from time to time devastate crops in Africa. And who can forget the painted ladies of last summer. They started in Morocco and swarmed in huge numbers right across Europe, all the way to Iceland. In a 2-hour period on 30th May people who specialise in this sort of thing estimated that 15 million were in England and Wales alone. Painted ladies even put in an appearance on St Kilda, the outer-most of the Outer Hebrides where they were the first butterflies to be seen for 2 years.

December 2009.

Nature Matters

Mid-winter thoughts

Very often supermarkets and suchlike try to make their car-parks slightly less dreary by planting them up with shrubs. Favourites are ever-greens such as pyracanthus, viburnum, holly or cotoneaster, all of which have berries and therefore provide a rich source of mid-winter food for birds. Those first to the feast are blackbirds, thrushes, finches and starlings all of which are used to the urban bustle and are therefore at home in such a setting. But just occasionally the mob is joined by exotic visitors from arctic Scandinavia called waxwings. These birds are about the size of a starling and, like starlings, move around in winter in large flocks.

They are a warm cinnamon-grey with a striking black band through the eye and a conical crest, a bit like a base-ball cap worn back-to-front.

The name waxwing comes from strange waxy red blobs on the tips of their secondary wing-feathers. Most years a few appear along the east coast anywhere from north Scotland to Essex but every so often the berry crop back home runs out early and waxwings flood in to this country from across the North Sea in search of food. On these occasions they come in such large numbers that birders talk about an irruption. The last irruption was in 2004 and the omens for a repeat this year are good. Flocks of several hundreds have been tracked all the way down from arctic Russia and began to arrive in Scotland in September. From there they have been spreading south and by early November several flocks of up to 60 birds each had reached East Anglia. Along with new arrivals, they can be expected to continue to roam around the south of England looking for any berries still on the shrubs. In March they will go home to nest. Their striking appearance and habit of forming large flocks makes it easy to see them and it's well worth keeping an eye open in case they are around. To get the latest news about their movements simply put "waxwing" into Google and Bob's your uncle!

Examples of the impact which climate change is having on the usual rhythms of nature come thick and fast. But what about this; the 25th November was a day of comparative calm after more than a week of pelting rain, high winds and general misery. There were even the odd shafts of sun; just enough, it seems, for a frog to utter a few feeble croaks from the direction of our pond. This rather suggests that he had checked in some weeks ago in the usual way to hibernate, had woken up thinking it was spring and was trying to make contact with a mate. In this he was not alone because a few days later another burst of sunshine was enough to get a great-spotted woodpecker in a neighbouring garden to make a half-hearted attempt to drum. This is his way of telling the local females that he's there and is something you would not usually expect to hear until February at the earliest.

I don't suppose there are many who really understand the science which underpins the debate about climate change, but this does not deny the rest of us the right to raise an eyebrow at some of the conclusions with which we are presented. For example take all this talk about cattle; we are told that cows produce between 8,000 and 10,000 litres of gas a day, most of which is methane, and that methane is 23 times more effective than carbon dioxide in trapping warm air from the earth. The conclusion is that if we all become vegetarians, we could do away with all the herds of beef-cattle and thereby make a valuable contribution in the war against global warming. But surely all that would happen is that we new vegetarians would take over the role as methane producers. I have shared this thought with a highly-qualified biochemist who broadly agrees but adds that because cows can digest cellulose and we can't we will never match their awesome output.

Thank goodness for that.

January 2010

Animals and snow

Animals have two big problems in snow; finding food and keeping warm. Small animals suffer more than large ones because their ratio of skin surface to body size is greater and therefore they lose heat faster. Also their stomachs are smaller which means that that they must eat frequently and choose food which has high nutritional value. Advertisements for bird-food make much of the nutritional value of their products and it is important to remember that kitchen scraps such as white bread when fed to small birds fill up their small crops with food which provides little energy. Larger birds such as pigeons are not faced with this problem to the same degree.

When food is short energy must be conserved. But hunting for food uses energy and the RSPB have recently issued guidance on how best to help birds in hard weather. In order to stress the importance of what they have to say, they remind us that bird populations were devastated by the cold winters of 1962 and '63. One point they stress is that we should avoid disturbing resting birds because to do so would cause them to fly and thus use up energy unnecessarily. Birds seem to know this and are tamer in cold weather. Kestrels conserve energy by watching for prey from perches rather than by hovering into a breeze which uses a great deal of energy.

Keeping warm is also a problem. Mammals grow thicker coats and some animals hibernate. The latter have evolved the ability to close down all but the most basic bodily processes and subsist throughout the winter on reserves of food built up in late summer. Butterflies native to cold-winter countries like ours hibernate in any of their four stages. Dormice hibernate as do bumble bees and reptiles. The Bumble Bee Trust recently expressed concern that the burrows where bees spend the winter may not be deep enough to withstand this year's extreme weather, which reminds me to tell you that I recently took a photograph on Fittleworth Common of a bumble bee flying over snow and about to re-enter it's burrow. Strange for an insect which should have been fast asleep.

In very cold weather badgers stay underground and nestle up to each other for warmth. The fug they generate melts surrounding snow and it is said that you can hear from outside the sound of their contented snores. When conditions are more to their liking they come out again to feed. Squirrels are the same except that they retire into winter dreys built for this purpose. Different dreys are used by the females to raise their families. Birds keep warm in various ways; some fluff up their feathers to trap air which helps to insulate their bodies, whilst others, usually the smaller ones, find somewhere cosy to snuggle up together for mutual warmth. Old nests are a favourite place, especially the domed ones built by wrens or long-tailed tits which can hold up to half a dozen birds stacked up on top of each other.

Of course when food is short birds are forced to search far beyond their usual range, something which puts birders on their toes. In the field next to us the snow has melted in the places where the cattle feed and the trampled-up earth is rich with insects. This provides an oasis for birds and the usual gang of rooks, crows and jackdaws has been joined by starlings, redwings, fieldfares, wagtails and surprisingly the odd lapwing. Also three visiting bullfinches have found buds on a honeysuckle to their taste. The Sussex bird website carries stories of similar movements, some involving rarities. But nothing to compare with the report from Wyncombe Close of a visit from a male snow bunting. These very distinctive birds (the males are mostly white with a black mantle and tail) are rare winter visitors. A few breed in Scotland but mostly they live further north. Their preferred winter habitat is the seashore and most years a few are seen along the Sussex coast. Just occasionally they come inland where they feed on berries and seeds. This is what the Wyncombe Close bird was doing. All very exciting!!

February 2010

Nature in art

Pre-historic cave paintings testify to man's enduring fascination with animals and it comes as no surprise that in the 16th century the old masters were quietly using wildlife subjects as background in pictures wherein the Catholic church ruled that religious themes must predominate. In such cases the animal often served as an emblem associated with the particular religious person shown in the picture but with the passing of time and, encouraged by exotic trophies brought back from foreign parts by explorers, the animal content grew until eventually these great artists were painting animal portraits pure and simple. However there was one problem; the artists were often painting subjects which they had never seen alive. Indeed many famous paintings were the work of artists using models which were stuffed skins and, unsurprisingly, the shape and poise were frequently wrong. The two pictures below make the point. They are both of a goldcrest; the one on the left was painted in about 1650 and was well-enough regarded at the time to be used as an illustration in a bird book. The one on the right was painted in 1915 by the famous wild-life artist Archibald Thorburn.

This same problem continued to confront wildlife artists into the early 19th century. Even the great American ornithologist and painter John James Audubon, whose monumental output included painting all the birds of the United States life-size in meticulous detail, relied heavily upon dead models and as a result much of his work, beautiful as it is, looks stilted and unnatural today. His English contemporary John Gould, who started life as a taxidermist and ornithologist, was himself an indifferent painter and much of his work was enhanced by his wife and by Edward Lear. The latter, although better known for his nonsense rhymes, was an excellent artist and one of the first to grasp the notion that wildlife is at its best when seen in places of great natural beauty and his paintings reflect this. Later artists were aided by the advent of binoculars and cameras which enabled them to capture vital detail in sketches made in the field from which finished work could be produced later. I have a book of unfinished pencil sketches done in the field by Archibald Thorburn, each simple line redolent of the grace and charm of a wild bird in a wild place. By contrast Beatrix Potter, also a wonderful artist, drew her animals to fit her stories; charming, wise and cuddly. Many future naturalists will have had their first meeting with animals in the pages of her books.

Others skilled as both illustrators and artists include Charles Tunnicliffe who illustrated *Tarka The Otter* and Frederick Frohawk who spent twenty years painting from life each of the four stages in the life of all the (then) 68 species of British butterflies. On a different scale Edwyn Lanseer's *Monarch of the Glen* immediately transports you to the wild moors of Scotland. Another of the same rank was Edward Wilson who perished at the age of 40 as a member of Captain Scott's ill-fated expedition to the Antarctic in 1912. Had he lived a full life his work would be better known today. Of the many excellent contemporary artists none is better than the Swedish painter, author and ornithologist Lars Jonsson who recently completed a guide to the birds of Europe for which he did the illustrations himself. Every bird is shown in all plumages for both sexes in the meticulous detail demanded by birders armed with to-day's state-of-the-art telescopes and cameras. Each picture is anatomically accurate and a work of art in its own right. Separately he has painted pictures of birds in the field which capture to perfection the cold light and sense of wilderness of his native Tundra. Always he aims to ask and answer the questions, where did his subject come from, why is it there and where is it going next?

All these painters, and many more, are first and foremost naturalists with a love for both their subjects and the places where they live. They are skilled equally as illustrators, and artists able, with understanding, sympathy and inspiration, to interpret the character of wild animals and paint them where nature meant them to be. Their work enriches us all.

March 2010

Nature Matters

Birds in spring

Of all the chirps, quacks, coos squawks and whistles which birds make, everyone's favourite is the trilling song of spring. And it comes from the males. The purpose is two-fold; the first is to tell the local females that they are there and up for a bit of family life, and second is to keep competing males off their patch. Viscount Grey recounts in his book *The Charm Of Birds* how he watched two male wrens with adjoining territories, both in full song. There appeared to be, he tells us, rules whereby the birds took it in turns to sing, the silent one listening attentively to the other and when his turn came, trying to out-do the first in volume and passion. And so it went on until their tiny bodies almost burst with the effort. The scene brings back memories of that wonderful song in the 1950s musical; *Annie Get Your Gun*; "Anything you can do I can do better....I can do any thing better than you"!!

Many of our resident birds, song thrushes, blackbirds, robins and suchlike, start to sing as early as January and from there things build up to a crescendo in April when the migrants arrive. This merry chorus lasts through until the beginning of July and then begins to peter out as the nesting season draws to a close. The thing which makes bird-song unique in the animal world is an organ in the throat equivalent to the larynx in mammals which is called the syrinx. It is situated at the point where the trachea forks into the lungs and enables birds to make two sounds at the same time, something which bestows upon birds great virtuosity both as songsters and mimics. Even so it is necessary for baby chicks to learn from their parents the call-notes appropriate to their species, something which, as in humans, often gives rise to the creation of regional accents. The human ear will not notice this but sophisticated recording equipment can spot it. Once learnt, these notes are firmly imprinted in their minds, but sometimes other ambient sounds also get picked up. There are a couple of amusing examples; the first concerns a species of bird of paradise, long thought to be extinct but which recently emerged from the depths of the jungle in Papua New Guinea with a call which it must have picked up in it's jungle isolation resembling a predator's growl. And the other is of a lyrebird which, in the 1930s, was kept by a farmer in Australia who passed the evenings playing tunes to it on his flute. After a while he released the bird back into the wild where it raised a family. with the result that there grew up and still exists 75 years and many generations later a local community of lyrebirds whose call includes flute-like sounds which replicate phrases from the tunes played by the farmer. And all this before we have even mentioned the best mimics of all; parrots!

Another thing chicks must learn early on is the ability to recognise their own species from amongst all the others they will later encounter as adults. This they do by bonding with their parents and siblings in the nest and by so doing they ensure that when their turn comes they confine their courting activities to their own species. What can happen if this goes wrong was first demonstrated by placing newly hatched linnet chicks in the nest of a canary where they were, of course, brought up by foster-parent canaries in a family of canaries. As a consequence these linnets, when adult, rejected other linnets and chose to raise their families instead with canaries. The result was pretty but inevitably sterile offspring.

So what about cuckoos which, famously, lay their eggs in the nests of other birds? Clearly it would not do if a baby cuckoo grew up to sing like, say, the pipit which fostered it and worse still if it were unable to recognise other cuckoos and tried instead to mate only with pipits. Yet it must rely upon its childhood memories to recognise a pipit as the potential foster parent for its own chicks. These are complex matters which still puzzle animal behaviourists. They suspect, but cannot prove, that the knowledge which enables a cuckoo to recognise where to lay its eggs is inherited and passes from generation to generation: and that by hearing the call of its real parents when a chick it learns to sort out with whom it should most profitably mate when its own turn comes round.

April 2010.

Nature Matters

In support of microbes

If the choice were to lie between a walk on a sunny summer day across the downs, larks singing, orchids in flower and the air fragrant with the smell of thyme; or, say, a trip to the Farne Islands at the end of June when puffins are flying in off the sea over cliffs pink with thrift, beaks full of sand-eels for their chicks: or a morning spent turning out the compost heap, I don't suppose the compost heap would attract many takers. Yet the microscopic bacteria, algae, yeasts and suchlike which inhabit a compost heap represent the largest proportion of life on our planet. Many are far too small to see with the naked eye but they have a huge impact upon the environment in which we live. Wherever vegetation or animal remains lie and rot, be it the woodland floor, hedgerow or untilled field, these micro-organisms are at work. Either by digestion or respiration they break down waste material and return it as the nutrient which sustains renewed growth. Gardeners construct a compost heap and ensure that the right conditions of moisture and ventilation prevail. Thereby they assist what is no more than a natural process.

The versatility of these same minute organisms has been used by mankind in many ways. Take yeast; in the presence of oxygen yeast produces as waste carbon dioxide just like us and this process is used by bakers to make bread rise. However without oxygen, a condition in which higher animals would not survive, yeast continues to live. The difference is that, instead of carbon dioxide, the waste is alcohol. This happy trick has enabled the Scots, for the best part of two centuries, to make a decent living by placing yeast in a vat of burn water drawn straight from the hillside which has been used to steep a mash of malted barley. Thus starts a process which leads to the golden nectar which oils the wheels of human discourse and spreads joy to all corners of the globe.

But back to the compost heap where the conditions produced by bacterial action and fostered by the gardener are also ideal for many other animals to live in. Some, such as hedgehogs and slowworms, find the warmth ideal for over-wintering. Others, such as grass snakes, lay eggs there, secure in the knowledge that they will be more or less safe from predators and will be kept at about the right temperature and humidity until ready to hatch. These eggs are about the size of a pigeon's egg and are soft-shelled and white. Adders give birth to live young for which purpose the females form a sort of colony, so there is no risk of confusion. I once found in my heap several young grass snakes about 3 inches long. The interesting thing was that they were only a couple of feet from some young slowworms which, being older, were bigger. When both are adult the snake would happily swallow the slowworm whole. Other inhabitants of a compost heap are woodlice, often mistaken for harmful insects but actually blameless terrestrial crustacea and thus related to lobsters, centipedes which are carnivores, millipedes which are herbivores and beetles.

Talking of which reminds me of something I read in the papers recently about a particular species of dung beetle, an insect which gets its name because the male makes a ball out of dung, rolls it huge (by beetle standards) distances before pushing it down a hole where its mate waits to insert her eggs. But occasionally an un-mated rival follows the rightful owner down the hole and this provokes a pushing match in the tunnel. The winner is rewarded by getting to be the father of the ensuing family and by this means the genes which ensure the strongest push are passed from generation to generation. As a result there has evolved over time a species of beetle so powerful that it can push an estimated 1,141 times its body-weight. It's a nice thought that if the forefathers of present-day men had been similarly tested we would by now be able to haul six fully-laden double-decker buses. And you only have to watch a rugby match at scrum-time and note the increase in the size of the pushing apparatus of the forwards since the game turned professional to see how easily this could come about.

May 2010

Nature Matters

Amazing rare things

Although it happened more than 25 years ago I can recall the scene as if it were yesterday. We were walking along a dry river bed in the foothills of the Atlas mountains, the early spring sun warm but not yet oppressive and the air full of birdsong. Bridget was pottering round looking for amethysts (if she found one she never let on) when I saw this butterfly. It was perched on a boulder, wings open and pressed hard down on the rock to soak up the warmth. Only the top-side was visible and the markings were typical of any medium-sized fritillary but nothing to suggest which particular one. So, camera at the ready, I crept closer until a slight movement caught its eye and made it lift its wings thereby exposing its underside markings. To my amazement it was a Queen of Spain fritillary, a butterfly of exquisite beauty which I had long gazed at in my books but never before seen. So excited was I by the vision in my viewfinder that I almost forgot to release the shutter and take the photograph.

When eventually I did here is the result; but of necessity I'm afraid only in black and white. What you see on the hind-wing as white blobs are really gleaming metallic silver markings set off against a background of delicate shades of brown. I had to wait another twenty years before seeing a Queen of Spain fritillary again, this time in the Pyrenees.

But now comes the exciting bit; three years ago out of the blue a number of these butterflies appeared in the countryside just north-west of Chichester and have been seen off and on thereabouts ever since. They have found a place where there are plenty of both wild and field pansies which their caterpillars need to feed on and are known to have bred and produced same-season adult offspring. But what is not certain is whether they have ever survived our winter or whether the colony is renewed each year by new migrants from the continent. These butterflies are unusual in that they can choose to hibernate in any of their four life-cycle phases according to needs. Last October they were seen laying eggs so, if they survived what turned out to be a very harsh winter there is a chance that we may soon be able to add this beautiful butterfly to our list of native Sussex fauna.

For our next piece of news we are indebted to our neighbours in Bignor who report having seen on two occasions recently a goshawk in the area of Bignor Hill. This bird of prey is much like a sparrow hawk in shape, colour and habits but is the size of a buzzard and is rated a national rarity. Interestingly there is an article in the current edition of The Sussex Wildlife Trust magazine about a pair of goshawks breeding in a secret location in West Sussex. We do not know if there is a link between the two reports but it would be nice if these splendid birds were to follow in the footsteps of buzzards, peregrines and red kites and become part of our local avifauna.

And finally there is the matter of the white stork which spent a few hours on the water at Douglaslake Farm on 22nd April. Janet Hester was the first to see it and was so astonished that she rang me for a second opinion. But there was no doubting its identity and when I reported it to the Sussex Ornithological Society their excitement was tempered only by the thought that it might have escaped from captivity rather than be a wild bird. By coincidence Chris Donne tells me that he had recently seen a very large bird flying high over the village. From his experience in Africa he believes it can only have been a crane or stork and indeed a couple of cranes were present at the Wiggonholt RSPB reserve just the day before. Extraordinary!

June 2010

White storks at a nest in Portugal.

Unravelling animal behaviour

The last few months have provided a good opportunity to see, often at close quarters, the family life of birds. Indeed several people in the village who have installed nesting boxes complete with cameras which can relay pictures from within onto their television screens have now become experts on such domestic matters as incubation, feeding the family and nest hygiene. But if the subjects are a species wherein the male and female are not easily told apart it can be difficult to keep track of everything that goes on. Take blue tits for example; the books tell us that the nest is built by both parents, that incubation is left entirely to mum who is fed on the nest by dad, and that both parents then feed the chicks, all of which paints a picture of idyllic family life. But complications can arise when, as often happens, a female visits a neighbour's nest and proceeds to lay an egg or two of her own without, apparently, the rightful owners raising any objection. Add to this the enthusiasm with which philandering males take time out from family duties to pursue other local females and it is easy to see how difficult it is to keep track of the exact genetic parentage of the brood being studied and how, indeed, it would add immensely to the jollity of observation if only one could tell one blue tit from another.

Those who wish to investigate these matters in more detail use leg-rings for identification and electronic tags to trace movement. And, of course, they keep meticulous records over long periods of time. As a result researchers are beginning to learn more about, for instance, what characteristics a bird inherits, what it learns by association early in life from its parents and what it learns through its own life-experience. How, for example, does a bird know if it should migrate and if so when and where to? In many cases the answer is that they simply follow their parents. Experiments have shown, however, that if the fledglings of a migrating species are separated from their parents before it is time to migrate and are relocated say 200 miles to the west, they will, bereft of parental guidance, migrate in the right direction but to a destination also 200 miles to the west of where you'd expect. This behaviour is held to be evidence that the bird is driven by an inherited instinct to migrate. The next spring, however they will return to the place where they were born, drawn, it seems, by an impulse imprinted upon them as a chick. But then next autumn they follow their own life-experience and return to the same "wrong" winter destination as the previous year and this routine is maintained ever after.

Researchers have also tested the proposition that all birds of the same species have the same ability to do clever things. Crows are generally thought to be the smartest of all birds, a good example of which occurs in a race of crow found in New Caledonia. Their party-piece is the ability to use a stick, preferably one with a hook in the end to reach otherwise inaccessible food. If presented with a short length of wire they will even fashion the hook for themselves. But the interesting bit is this; only a proportion of the crow population have the innate ingenuity and wit to work out how to do this for themselves. However other less astute crows acquire the ability by watching and imitating the clever ones whilst those remaining, the largest section of the population as it happens, are either too lazy or too thick even to try. Presumably Darwin's laws of natural selection will eventually cause their elimination.

Most of these studies are conducted by highly trained field workers. Norman Travers, however, was a man who got to know animals as much by intuition and empathy as anything else. After the war, in which he was awarded an M.C. for rescuing a comrade trapped in a burning tank, he settled in Rhodesia (later Zimbabwe) and took to farming and, after a while, to wildlife conservation. He defied conventional practice to build up nationally important populations of rhinos, buffalos and elephants. His relationship with animals is best illustrated by the diverse assembly that accompanied him and his wife on their walks in the countryside; a lion (whose pelt, after its death, was to hang on the wall of his house), a hyena, a warthog, an otter, two Labradors, a dachshund and a cat were typical. In March this year Mr Travers died aged 88 and The Times gave him a full-page obituary which started with these words;

> *"Only the elephants could have delivered such a moving tribute to*
> *Norman Travers. Shortly before he was buried on*
> *his farm in eastern Zimbabwe two forty-year-old bulls arrived*
> *unbidden, wandered through the crowd of 250 mourners, lumbered up*
> *to the coffin and sniffed it long and intently.*
>
> *When the last spadeful of earth had been cast upon the grave, they*
> *stood together on the heap of ground he lay beneath. Three times in*
> *the ensuing week they returned and stood by the grave".*

July 2010.

Nature Matters

A wonderful place for birds

History tells us that in 1876 Pagham Harbour was sealed off from the sea and drained. The purpose was to provide additional land for agriculture and protect the local church from the encroaching sea. But 34 years later storm-damage caused renewed flooding and, as a result, we have today an area of some 616 hectares consisting of tidal water, saltmarsh, mudflats, shingle, reedbeds and swamp. Small wonder, then, that the place is rated amongst the best in the county for birds and is designated a Site Of Special Scientific Interest which is managed jointly by the Sussex Wildlife Trust and WSCC.

There are three ways to get onto the reserve. The simplest is to drive through Pagham, down Church Lane and park at the end. A short walk through a gate and down a track takes you to the north wall along which runs a path which divides the mudflats and saltings from a large pool fringed by reed-beds and water-meadows. This is a magical place for birds, especially in the winter when huge flocks of brent geese, wigeon and godwits are interspersed with curlew, little egrets, herons, teal, pintails and little grebes. At low tide the saltings are alive with small waders and occasionally seals haul themselves up on the far bank. Keen birders form small groups and scan flocks through their telescopes for rarities but in no way intrude upon the peacefulness sought by those who wish no more than to enjoy a beautiful place in harmony with nature and have no great need to put a name to everything they see.

Another way into the reserve is to take the road which leads down to Pagham beach. Turn right at the roundabout in front of the Beach Café (where, if nothing else, the all-day breakfast alone makes the trip to down there worthwhile) and follow the lane through holiday bungalows until you come to a car park on The Spit. From there a short walk along the shingle towards the sea quickly leads you into what, in summer, is a virtual paradise of wild flowers; valerian, bugloss, clumps of blue-green sea-kale and horned poppies, all set off against carpets of bright yellow stonecrop. We were there recently and an extra excitement was provided by a peregrine falcon which spent some minutes spooking a family of oystercatchers.

To explore the west side of the reserve it's best to take the road to Selsey and a mile before you get there turn off to Church Norton. On the way you can call in at Sidlesham Visitor's Centre where there is a hide which gives views over Ferry Pool. This stretch of fresh-water is a magnet for unusual birds, especially in the migrating season and in the winter you would be unlucky not to see avocets, the Suffolk colony of which featured in this year's television *Spring-watch*. However a busy road with lorries thundering past separates the hide from the pool so this is a place simply to see birds rather than spend time. Better to move on quickly to Church Norton where you can park by the church and walk out to the shore. Little and Sandwich terns will be there in summer and in winter slavonian grebes are often bobbing about out at sea whilst turnstone, ringed plover and redshank are just three of the many waders which feed amongst the seaweed at low-tide.

And now something different; this year a lot of butterflies have appeared with their usual markings partially obscured by a dusting of dark pigments, a condition caused by extreme temperatures coinciding with the time when caterpillars are pupating and soft tissue is vulnerable. Those seen locally include white admirals, small tortoiseshells, commas and even purple emperors. The effect can be quite dramatic so it's worth keeping an eye open. Another strange occurrence this summer has been the unusual number of female silver-washed fritillaries which carry the rare gene which makes them olive-green rather than the usual rich brown. This form is called Valezina and such is the beauty of the insect that the famous Victorian entomologist, Frederick Frohawk, gave the name to his youngest daughter. This lady was later to marry into the nobility and as Valezina, Viscountess Bolingbroke, lived in Pulborough well into the early 1980s, her name redolent of the sun-lit woodland glades and the rare and majestic butterfly which inspired it.

August 2010

Nature Matters

Summer memories

It was late in May and we were walking along a downland track above North Stoke. Up until then the weather had been, at best, patchy but that day the smell of spring was in the air. It was too early for orchids but both red and white campion, vetch, and trefoil were amongst the flowers providing colour. Larks were singing and every so often we could hear, away in the distance, the call of a yellow hammer. The big surprise, though, was finding a mole out of its burrow quietly snuffling around amongst the leaf-litter, looking for things to eat. It took absolutely no notice of us even when we closed in to take photographs.

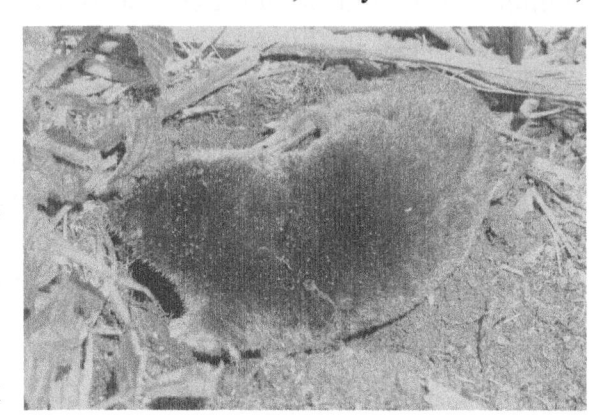

May was when a white stork came briefly to Fittleworth, cranes were at Wiggonholt and a spoonbill spent a few days at Pagham. Buzzards were nesting nearby and are now the most frequently-seen raptor in the neighbourhood. There are still whispers of goshawks not far away and an osprey on its annual journey from Africa north-bound spent most of June at Burton Mill Pond and was once seen in aerial combat with a buzzard. In recent years ospreys have extended their breeding range southwards so maybe this bird will come again next year with a mate. So anglers beware!!

In spring and early summer there was enough rain to ensure a good showing of wild flowers. Bluebells did especially well in the woods around Coates Common and if the wild daffodils in Stopham Woods were not quite so picturesque as sometimes this was probably because recent coppicing has temporarily robbed the vistas of the dappled light which makes these woods so special in spring. Then there is Kithurst Hill where there is a meadow which still resembles what so much of the Downs was like 60 years ago. In spring it is carpeted with cowslips, wild thyme and clover, all with that special sharp colour which typifies chalk-downland flowers. Butterflies include small blues and Dukes of Burgundy, the latter the only European representative of a family more often found in Central America. As summer unfolds orchids, marjoram, hemp agrimony, hairbells knapweed, scabious and rampion provide nectar for the butterflies prominent amongst which are pretty chalkhill blues.

It is fashionable these days to attribute anything unusual which occurs in nature to climate change. But was it this that caused the black-tailed godwits which we saw at Pagham on 6th July to return from their nesting grounds in the tundra so ridiculously early that they were still in the breeding plumage which we normally never see in this country? Their exceptionally deep chestnut colour suggested that they belonged to the race which comes from Iceland, so might not their early return have been to escape the recent volcanic dust? Another thing for which it is difficult to blame climate change concerns those butterflies which habitually fit in two generations per season. With these it is increasingly the case that the second generation is now the more prolific. This is especially so with wood whites, an endangered species now largely confined to the woods north of Kirdford and one for which the word dainty might have been invented. A couple of weeks ago I found one on Ebernoe Common where reports had suggested they had recently established a tenuous foothold. Wood whites have a courtship routine which is unique in the world of butterflies. What happens is this; first the couple stand face to face, the tips of their antennae gently touching. Then the male uncurls his proboscis as he would if he were about to sip nectar from a flower and proceeds to wave it like a wand above the lady's head. If she has eggs to lay this odd ceremony can last for up to five minutes If she has not, she soon flies off and that's that.

And finally something which would have caused a buzz amongst butterfly collectors of an earlier generation; the appearance in nearby Southwater Woods of a silver-washed fritillary which was a bilateral gynandromorph. This rare condition is caused by a mal-function in the X-chromosome which determines gender and in a simpler form results in a butterfly which shows a random mix of male and female markings. But the much rarer bilateral gynandromorph is one in which there is an abrupt division down the middle of its body, everything on one side being male and on the other female. In the field these anomalies only show up in species where there is a visible difference in the wing markings between the genders. This defect is one to which insects are more exposed than mammals because, in their case, the X-chromosome affects the growth of the whole body, so there is much that can go wrong. In mammals, however, it only affects organs directly concerned with reproduction which then secrete the hormones which stimulate the development of the secondary characteristics associated with gender; beards, deep voices and suchlike.

September 2010

A brief look at evolution

The eyes of most birds are positioned so that they look straight along their beaks. This enables them to take careful aim at anything they wish to grab or peck. But if such a bird is one which feeds by dipping its beak vertically into mud it will find its field of view restricted to the bit of ground just under its face, a situation which carries the risk of ambush. Snipe feed like this and have solved the problem by evolving eyes which are placed well back in their skulls, thereby enabling them to scan the horizon even when their beaks point down. Other birds which feed the same way have evolved different strategies to ensure their safety; curlews, for example, have a long, downward-curving beak which enables them to probe the mud without looking down. Avocets achieve the same thing by wading in shallow water and using an upward-curved beak to stir up food with side-ways sweeps. Others feed in groups so there is always at least one pair of eyes to watch out for danger. Nut and seed eaters, such as finches, have short, stubby beaks for maximum strength and those which tear meat from bone have short hooked beaks.

All this is just one very small example of the way by which living things have developed physical characteristics which help them to survive, a process made possible because, within any species of animal or plant, there are always minute differences which are specific to each individual. If this difference is to the advantage of the individual and is part of its DNA it will be passed on to its off-spring. Thus in time a new and fitter strain will develop which will prevail at the expense of those without the characteristic. Thus there is in the natural world a mechanism constantly at work which weeds out the weak and favours the strong: a process, in other words, of natural selection and the survival of the fittest.

Life on Earth can be traced back to more than 3600 million years ago. Such a number baffles the mind and is more easily comprehended if re-scaled to just one year. Each day would then represent 10 million years. On such a calendar we would find at the beginning of January a planet stinking of sulphur belched up from volcanoes, and an atmosphere which would be lethal to present-day life. Only the simplest microscopic bacteria existed and it was not until they acquired chlorophyll and were able to photosynthesise their own food did plant-life begin to flourish. Even so, we must wait until September before we find things even as simple as colonies of single-cell organisms, each capable of individual survival but linked together by minute hooks which were forerunners of present-day sponges. By mid-November sea-dwellers were coming onto dry land, changing their fins into limbs and becoming the first reptiles. Some climbed into the trees and those which were able to, jumped and then glided from branch to branch. Soon their scales changed to feathers and archaeopteryx, (primitive birds) joined the party.

Early on Christmas day (63 millions ago on our imaginary calendar), there was a dramatic cooling of the planet which wiped out egg-laying dinosaurs and allowed mammals which retain their embryos within their bodies until they are ready to be born and then continue to suckle them from milk-secreting glands, to dominate. Tree-dwelling primates left the forests and came out onto the plains, stood up on their hind legs and by the early evening of New Year's Eve early-mankind was established. By mid-night that same day, this new species had changed the nature of vast tracts of Earth's surface and developed the diverse pattern of cultures and civilisations which we know today.

During all this time, by a series of minute steps, life-forms of all kinds have diversified and found ways to exist in every corner of the planet. Cataclysmic changes in the environment have, from time to time, wiped out swathes of animals and plants but those that survived have replaced them. And all through this, bacteria very similar to those from which all else is descended continue to exist around the lips of volcanoes where the sulphurous atmosphere replicates conditions as they were when life first began.

Although evolution is driven primarily by physical changes which are passed from generation to generation by genes, there is evidence that patterns of behaviour acquired during a life-time and passed on, probably by off-spring copying their parents, can eventually become instinctive. Why otherwise would our dog, despite many generations of refinement and gentrification, still take any opportunity to roll in anything sufficiently smelly to mask his own scent if it were not some primeval instinct to disguise himself and thereby escape the attention of his long-departed enemies?

October 2010

Brownsea Island re-visited

Brownsea Island lies in the middle of Poole Harbour which is the second largest natural harbour in the world. (It is mildly irritating, especially with the Ashes looming, that Sydney is the largest.) A small ferry leaves from the wharf just beside the terminus where the chain-ferry comes in from Sandbanks and during the ten-minute crossing we were able to see at close quarters some of the multi-million-pound houses on the Poole waterfront which makes this one of the most expensive places in the world to live. Add to this the never-ending bustle of commercial sea traffic and pleasure boats and Poole is not an obvious place to go in search of wildlife – except that on the western side of the harbour lies a vast expanse of wetland and saltmarsh, beyond which are the lowland heaths of Arne and Purbeck, the whole combining to form an integrated area as rich in beauty and as varied in flora and fauna as any in north Europe.

Back, then, to Brownsea; owned by the National Trust and with a small Nature Reserve managed with unfussy efficiency by the Dorset Wildlife Trust, there is a range of habitats sufficient to interest any naturalist. Our visit was early in September and time was short so we concentrated on the lagoon where the selection of water-birds never fails to thrill. There are three hides which give excellent views over the lagoon and reed-beds. One is reached by covered walk-way and puts you right in amongst the little islets upon which both sandwich and little terns nest. A visit in early summer when family life is in full swing would be a treat indeed. Instead early autumn is when winter flocks are beginning to build up and passage migrants pass through. We saw a couple of rare little curlew sandpipers on their way from Arctic Siberia where they bred to Africa to spend the winter. About the size of a blackbird, they get their name by virtue of a beak which curves down like a miniature curlew. The male was still in his pinkish breeding plumage and looked very smart as the pair of them fed in the shallow water just in front of our hide. Others said they'd also seen ruffs, medium-sized waders which can be difficult to identify unless the males are in their very distinctive breeding plumage. This consists of frilly collar and chest feathers the colours of which vary from bird to bird. At mating time the males assemble at special places for a ceremony called the lek in which chest feathers are fluffed up for maximum effect. There is much dancing and, as things heat up vicious fights break out. Meanwhile the much smaller females in drab brown plumage stand demurely to one side until the males have sorted themselves out.

They reckon that some 3000 avocets, a quarter of our entire native population, over-winter on the Brownsea lagoon and already there was a vast flock resting on a mudflat out in the middle with single birds feeding close enough to enable us to watch the way in which they use their upward-curved beaks to sift the water for food. I can remember when, as a schoolboy already intrigued by the ways of birds, areas of East Anglia which had been off-limits to civilians during the war were, in 1947, re-opened to visitors and two pairs of breeding avocets were discovered. The species had not been seen in this country for more than a hundred years and the excitement was intense. The birds were thought to have come over from Holland and were taking advantage of the changes in fenland water-levels which were a result of wartime coastal defences. The RSPB were at the time building up their new reserve at nearby Minsmere and decided to replicate the habitat by constructing their now-famous Scrape. At first this attracted only a few birds but conservationists persevered and from this small beginning these stylish birds now turn up anywhere around the English coast where there are expanses of muddy shallow water suited to their way of feeding.

Another highlight that day was seeing a flock of 15 spoonbills, another water-bird which is expanding into this country from Holland. After an absence of about three hundred years a pair bred again in 1990 at a secret location in East Anglia and since then numbers have increased each year. Spoonbills are heron-sized pure white birds and get their names from their huge spatulate beaks which also give them rather a goofy look. Until, that is, you see a flock of them in flight as we did. Then their huge white wings alternately gliding and beating, primaries outlined against a bright blue sky and huge, slightly down-curved beaks stretched out in front, is a sight to cherish.

November 2010

Nature Matters

Wild geese and an elusive butterfly

They reckon that some 700,000 geese come down from the far north to over-winter at various places around the coast of the British Isles. They are made up of six different species and come from places as far apart as Canada, Greenland, Iceland Scandinavia and Arctic Russia. Essential habitats are mudflats, estuaries and saltmarshes with a hinterland of wet meadows. These are the places where they can graze by day and roost, often on water, at night. Each species has its favourite place to which it returns year after year and should not be confused with those other species which are here all year round. Of these Canada geese are the most numerous. Introduced here by King Charles II in 1678, they still carry the stigma of being ornamental rather than truly wild birds. Other residents are graylags which sometimes come onto the water-meadows which border the Rother and Arun and a growing number of feral Egyptian geese which recently started to nest in Petworth Park.

The only truly wild geese which visit our stretch of coast in any numbers in the winter are dark bellied brents. However what we lack in variety we make up for in quantity with Chichester harbour alone providing mid-winter counts in excess of 10,000 birds. Like all visiting geese, brents have undertaken an epic journey to get here. The birds pair for life and families stay together until they are ready to breed. When migrating they fly in a "V" formation which enables each bird to benefit from the buoyancy created by the wing-movement of the bird in front with senior birds taking turns to lead. By flying thus a group can keep going 70% longer than a single bird on its own. This helps if you weigh as much as a goose.

Once here the birds stay in tight groups. Scouts are sent out to find the best feeding grounds and sentinels appointed to keep watch for trouble. It sometimes happens that their route south has taken them close to the territory of a different species of goose destined to migrate elsewhere. As a consequence a few individuals may inadvertently become integrated into the wrong flock and get carried along to the wrong destination. When this happens the interloper appears to mix in quite happily. I have, for example, seen barnacle geese grazing amongst the brents at Pagham whilst its friends had probably settled in for the winter up around the Solway Firth.

Geese share their habitat with huge numbers of other waterfowl such as duck, swans, waders, grebes and herons. Many have come, like the geese, to spend the winter here from far off places and it has always seemed to me that, knowing where all these birds have come from and why, adds an extra layer of enjoyment to being amongst them. And if you are there at dawn or dusk when the cold winter light is at its best and they take wing in their noisy hundreds to move between feeding grounds and night-time roost, you are promised a spectacle described by the bird artist and founder of the Wildfowl and Wetland Trust, Peter Scott, as one of the most thrilling in the whole world of nature.

As we approach mid-winter it seems appropriate to finish these notes with a tale from last summer. It concerns brown hairsteaks, smallish but extremely pretty butterflies. Sadly, though, they are seldom seen, partly because they are quite scarce and partly because they spend most of their lives perched high up on tree-tops. They are the last of our native butterflies to hatch and enthusiasts are to be seen in mid-August standing for hours in likely spots, binoculars at the ready without ever seeing anything. I have only ever seen a brown hairstreak three times and on each occasion it was out of range of my camera. So the taking of a decent photograph of this elusive insect has been a long-held ambition…..until, that is, last August when on a sunny Sunday afternoon after a good lunch eaten in the garden I saw out of the corner of my eye a butterfly flitting around on a near-by flowerbed. At first I dismissed it lazily as nothing more than a late-hatching gate-keeper but then something about it made me take a closer look. And guess what!! It was my longed-for brown hairstreak, a female so perfect that it must just have hatched. So I went and got my camera, checked that the lens was correct and, with that mounting sense of excitement which comes when a once-in-a-lifetime opportunity is in the offing, went back out to investigate. The butterfly had by now settled on a cosmos flower the colour of which set off to perfection the golden browns and fine silver tracery of its wings. I got several photos before it moved off to a nearby myrtle shrub. Better still; now it had perched side-on at eye-level in a pose which captures superbly the delicate elegance of a butterfly sipping nectar from blossom: in other words all the ingredients for the perfect photograph. I had plenty of time to snap away from various angles before the butterfly finally flew off and out of the garden, gone for ever. But who cares!! I had what I wanted, perhaps a dozen or more pictures and by the law of averages a few at least must be okay. So I went inside to the comfort of a chair to review the results, pressed the playback button and there they were on the screen, bright, clear, pin-sharp, and perfectly centred; the fateful words "NO CARD INSERTED."

December 2010

Surviving winter

A basic requirement for all animals is an adequate supply of nutritious food. This is specially so when the weather turns cold and both finding food and keeping warm requires more calories. Small animals suffer even more because they loose heat faster and are therefore obliged to eat more frequently. A bird the size of a blue tit must eat food rich in calories continuously throughout the short daylight hours of winter just to last through the night. To combat all these problems animals have evolved various strategies. The most obvious is that they time the birth of their young to coincide with spring when much-needed food is most plentiful. But once families are raised and winter approaches provision must be made for the hard times ahead. Birds have the advantage of being extremely mobile and some use this facility to depart for a warmer place. Others which have spent the summer high up in the north come down here to enjoy what to them is a more hospitable climate and these make up a large proportion of our winter bird population. Many arrive over the North Sea and their over-riding concern once here is to find enough to eat. If there is sufficient in the north-east they stay there and if not they spread out in search of more and it is at such times that we in the south see them.

Some other animals have evolved the ability to hibernate. This involves building up body-fat reserves in late summer sufficient to enable the animal to snuggle down and go into a sleep the duration and depth of which varies from one species to another. Dormice, for example, build a winter nest, roll up into a ball and allow respiration, heart rate and temperature to fall. Muscles become rigid and a state of torpor lasts from September until April. All our native reptiles (snakes and lizards) and amphibians (newts, frogs and toads) hibernate as do most of our insects. Butterflies do so either as adults, eggs, caterpillars or pupae according to species. The worst thing that can happen to an animal in deep hibernation is that it wakes up prematurely either because it has been disturbed or because the weather is unseasonably warm. If this happens either the shock will kill it stone dead or it will start to move around and use up reserves of food which it will be unable to replace. Others go into a partial hibernation from which they can awaken temporarily if conditions allow. Examples are badgers, hedgehogs, all mice except dormice and bats. Others such as foxes, deer and rats simply tough it out, some, habitually above the snow-line, turning white to escape detection.

Although the list of bird species which come to the south of England each winter remains more or less the same, their numbers vary considerably. Waxwings, starling-sized birds from Scandinavia which are a reddish-buff colour and have a striking crest, are a good example. A few come here every year and usually stray no further inland than the east coast. But every so often large flocks sweep across the country searching for berries to eat. These invasions occur when a good breeding season coincides with a poor berry crop at home. Early signs are that this year might be a good one for waxwings; they were first seen in the east of Scotland late in September and by late November they were turning up in various places to the north-east of a line approximately stretching from east Kent to Merseyside. The recent hard weather will inevitably push them further in our direction and this opens up the prospect of sightings here before winter is over. These birds move in flocks and their urban habits often lead them to feed from the berry-bearing shrubs so often planted to soften the scene around supermarket car-parks. One observer has even noted a preference for the plantings favoured by stores belonging to the Morrison group.

Other winter visitors are often of the same species as our own residents and it can be difficult to pick out which is which; wood pigeons, blackbirds and chaffinches are just a few in this category. However in the case of chaffinches visitors usually stay in flocks and feed on beech-mast whereas our native birds are solitary. It is always worth casting an eye over these flocks to see if they include a few bramblings, near relatives of chaffinches but more brightly coloured. They sometimes get caught up with migrating chaffinches and end up coming here with them. Bramblings have bullfinch-like white rumps which makes them easy to pick out.

Winter's relentless search for food often obliges animals to throw caution to the wind and do unusual things. Thus it was that last January the snow forced huge numbers of fieldfares and redwings to abandon open fields, where they often pass unnoticed, and come into urban areas where they were seen by everyone. Likewise, we had the extraordinary sight of a pair of foxes working our hedgerow for sheltering birds whilst several lapwings, fugitives, no doubt, from the frozen water-meadows along the river, were peacefully rummaging for food in the sludge around the cattle-troughs just a few yards away.

January 2011

Fireside musings

At the bottom of our road was a gate which led into a wood and the last house had a large rambling garden with lots of apple trees. Although I was only six years old I can still remember those trees because in the summer the branches were festooned with muslin bags in which were the caterpillars of eyed hawk-moths. The owner, a retired doctor, was a keen entomologist and allowed me and my brother (who is five years my senior and was therefore the trail-blazer in such adventures) to help move the bags so that the caterpillars always had fresh leaves to eat. We learned that during the month that it takes the newly-hatched caterpillar to grow into a bright green 2½ inch-long adult with a rather scary blue horn at its rear end, it sheds its skin four times to allow for growth. Then, when ready to pupate, it crawls down the trunk of the tree and buries itself a couple of inches deep in earth which we had prepared for the purpose. After a few days the pupa would have formed and we then popped it into a cage where it would remain for the next 10 months. During that time, in one of the great miracles of nature, the mushy goo within transformed itself into a beautiful brown and pink hawk-moth with large "eyes" on its hindwings. These it used to startle attackers. We would breed through dozens of moths each year, eventually releasing them to lay eggs on the same apple trees and start the process all over again.

Occasionally the kindly doctor allowed us to accompany him on an expedition into the woods which lay beyond his garden. There he taught us to recognise speckled woods, white admirals, silver-washed fritillaries, the occasional purple emperor and much else besides. I still have the little butterfly book which I had been given and, when I look at it to-day, it seems that I must have allowed myself quite a lot of latitude when ticking off what I imagined I had seen. Be that as it may, one thing which is beyond doubt is that these early adventures opened for me a window into the world of nature which has provided a source of pleasure ever since.

These memories came back to me the other day whilst reading a book I got for Christmas written by Patrick Barkham a feature-writer in *The Guardian*. Smitten by an obsession with butterflies at an early age and, now 35, he had decided to revive an unfulfilled ambition which he and his father had shared some years earlier, namely to see each of the 59 species listed as occurring in Britain, all in one season. (By selecting 2009, he actually knocked off an extra one making it 60 by visiting the small colony of migrant Queen of Spain fritillaries which had temporarily established itself near Chichester). His achievement owed quite a lot to help received from members of the Sussex Butterfly Trust and this set me to wonder how many species one might expect to see within a radius of say 20 miles of Fittleworth. Such a sweep would include the Downs, the fruitful heaths just west of Midhurst, and a decent selection of local woods up to the Surrey border. With a little determination and a modicum of luck I reckon that this should yield about 44 of the 59 species on the British list. But of course, a project like this requires reasonable identification skills and a knowledge of what habitat a particular butterfly lives in and when it flies.

Accurate identification and meticulous record-keeping are, of course, a necessary part of all conservation work. But failure to put a name to something seen still leaves much else to enjoy. For instance, take dragonflies, insects which when perched are of such elegance that, if they were plants, gardeners would use them for their architectural effect. But identification can drive you mad. Colour changes with age and the ranges of regional variations overlap. Add to this the fact that distinguishing features are often hard to see in the field and it becomes obvious that identification is best left to the experts. But this need not diminish the pleasure of watching them flitting in and out of waterside flowers in high summer. With iridescent wings and brightly coloured bodies shining in the sun, eyes that can see in all directions at the same time and the ability to fly in any direction simply by tilting their wings, it is easy to see how dragonflies are so well adapted to their environment that they have survived pretty well unchanged since before dinosaurs ruled the roost.

February 2011

Nature Matters

The first stirrings of spring

It was still only mid-January and already the black-headed gulls, so often seen around municipal rubbish dumps, were changing into their summer plumage complete with the black heads implied by their name. Then, a couple of days later, a somewhat precocious male great spotted woodpecker was tapping on the side of a tree to tell the girls that it was time for them to come and get him. Next thing, a queen bumblebee was coming out of the hole where she had spent the winter and flying off to find a place to lay eggs. The first of these will hatch into non-breeding worker bees and form the basis of a new colony. Later when the new colony is established her eggs start to hatch into males and females which fly off to mate with those from other colonies. As cold weather approaches all the workers and males die off, leaving fertile queens to hibernate and start things off all over again the following year.

All this and much more were signs that even though much of January and February was wet, cold and gloomy, nature was already preparing for the annual business of procreation. And once started things gathered pace. In February frogs return to ponds to find mates and spawn. Rooks abandon their winter roosts and return to rookeries to reclaim last year's nests. Those built with green sticks will have survived the winter best and noisy squabbles break out over possession. Add to this the nuisance caused by unpaired males trying to pinch the females of established couples and the whole scene is one of perpetual turmoil and squawking. But this quickly quietens once eggs are laid. Even then the male stands sentinel beside the nest to defend his domain from opportunistic raiders.

As February proceeds many of our resident birds will already be in song and have paired off. By March they are either building nests or already sitting on eggs. Birds like blue tits which feed their young on caterpillars delay egg-laying until they can be sure that the caterpillar-bearing trees are in leaf. Talking of which, blue tits now seem to be by far the most numerous birds visiting our feeders and this causes me to wonder whether they are benefiting from the misfortunes of greenfinches, so often the bully-boys of the bird-table and now suffering from trichomonosis. Although we are only on the fringe of this outbreak, it is rife in the south-west where numbers of greenfinches have crashed by a third. Chaffinches and dunnocks are also suffering but to a lesser extent.

For many people spring is epitomized by the sound of a skylark singing high above its mate whilst she sits tight on her nest below. Often it can be hard to tell larks from pipits but a rule of thumb is that pipits seldom reach heights of more than 60 feet whilst larks are usually twice that height. The young of both are born blind and naked whereas those of most ground-nesting birds can run around and feed themselves within hours of hatching. This, of course, exposes them to risks from predators. To counter this their mothers have learnt a neat trick whereby they distract would-be attackers; by dropping a wing and pretending to be injured, the mother leads the attacker away from her young. Then when she judges that the deception is complete and the young are safely hidden she flies off, leaving the attacker empty-handed.

And finally our picture was taken from her kitchen window by our daughter, Sarah, who lives near Cobham in Surrey. To her astonishment she recently saw these rose-ringed parakeets feeding at her bird-table. These birds came originally from the Himalayas and have been spreading slowly across the middle east and Europe. There is a well-established colony in Richmond Park and sporadically elsewhere in the south. But only a few couples each year have ever been seen in Sussex.

March 2011

Nature Matters

Ants, goldfinches and fossils

First a piece of information which might come in handy at one of these quiz competitions which crop up from time to time; if you were to put all the ants and termites which live in tropical South America into a heap their body-mass would exceed that of all other animals in the region combined. And that includes people. I read this the other day but also remember being told it some 20 years ago by a Venezuelan zoologist who was doing work in the upper reaches of the Orinoco. He was prompted to tell me by the sight of my poor wife who had just inadvertently trodden on a rotting mango and was frantically swiping at the invading horde of ants already half way up her leg.

There is little reason to lump termites and ants together. Indeed where their distribution overlaps ants are termite's biggest enemy. Termites are related to cockroaches and are confined mostly to the tropics, whereas ants are related to wasps and bees and inhabit both temperate and tropical areas. But they do have remarkably similar life-styles. Both live in large colonies numbering up to several million insects. These colonies have developed famously sophisticated societies consisting of a few individuals which breed and the rest, the workers, which undertake all the tasks necessary to maintain a viable community. With some, teams of workers undertake specialist tasks and have developed physical attributes to match; aggressive soldiers to fight, porters to forage for food and so on. Some tend the young larvae by keeping them at the correct temperature and there are those which can turn their hands to anything. Some can even take to breeding if needs be. They do this by lapping up hormones excreted by females which activate their normally dormant reproductive organs; surely the supreme act of multi-tasking!

The extraordinary success of termites and their reputation as dreaded pests derive in part from their ability to digest cellulose. Most termites do this with the assistance of bacteria in their gut. But some out-source the task to micro-fungi which they cultivate in gardens kept within their nests. Each species of termite has its own type of fungus, none of which are found anywhere else in the world. Typically the termite chews up and swallows cellulose-rich food and then excretes it undigested onto the fungus. The fungus in turn reduces it to a digestible compost which the termites then feed to their larvae.

Here on the south side of the village we recently became frustrated by never seeing the goldfinches which everyone else seemed to be getting on their feeders. So we took ourselves off to the Garden Centre and bought some nyger seed and the special feeder which they require. For nearly four weeks nothing much happened and then, out of the blue, a pair turned up and have been in constant attendance ever since. By contrast Mavis Sinclair over in

Wiggonholt got her first goldfinches within a few days of offering nygar seed. By now our pair has been joined by a siskin which, despite being much smaller, prefers to fight for one of the two nygar feeding holes rather than do what siskins usually do and feed upside down on the nearby nut feeder. All this makes me wonder whether we may in time attract redpolls and linnets. Both, after all, eat the same seed in the same way and there are plenty of them about in the surrounding countryside. Our predilection as a nation for feeding birds is well illustrated by the way that during the recent hard weather people who struggled to get out of their front gates somehow managed to maintain supplies of bird-food. We now as a nation spend £200 million a year on products related to bird-welfare which is much the same as gardeners spend on potting compost.

For many years scientists have pondered upon what caused birds to grow feathers. This may not be the hottest story in town but nevertheless you might find it interesting. The conventional wisdom has been that when reptiles sought the safety of trees and began to jump from branch to branch a strong survival benefit developed in favour of those which leapt the furthest. Thus scales turned to feathers and forelimbs were re-structured into wings. This belief strengthened in 1861 when German quarry workers found a 150-million year old fossil remains with feathers and forelimbs like a bird's wing but with reptilian claws and teeth. It was the size of a crow and was named archaeopteryx, the first-known bird. However in the past 30 years Chinese workers have unearthed fossil remains of reptiles which have clearly defined feathers but forelimbs which would have precluded flight. And they pre-date archaeopteryx by 5 million years. So the new theory is that terrestrial reptiles first developed feathers to assist them to run faster over the ground and then scuttled up into the trees where forelimbs turned to wings and they flew. In support of this theory is the similarity between the way these primitive feathers grew and the way that the down on present-day chicks is transformed into feathers. Perhaps this is just one more example of how the growth of animals between conception and adulthood can often re-trace their evolutionary history. Think of aquatic tadpoles turning into terrestrial frogs, toads and newts, or aquatic nymphs turning into airborne dragonflies. Or, indeed mammals, including us, whose embryos show vestiges of the gills which our ancestors millions of years ago needed to extract oxygen from the water in which they lived.

April 2011

Nature Matters

Things we may have missed

Each year teams of birders from The Sussex Ornithological Society get together for an event known as The Annual New Year Bird Race. The purpose is to see how many different birds each team can find in one day. I don't know any of the people involved but the write-up in the Society's quarterly Newsletter paints a picture of a group of good friends getting together to do what they enjoy most; going out into the countryside and looking for birds. But something else which comes through loud and clear is that these people are extremely competent birders. Their counts which number in the region of 150 different species in the day testify to an ability to identify just about everything they see no matter how unusual; and to see just about everything which is there. To get a feel for how difficult this is you only have to look in a guide book at the difference between, say, a willow tit and a marsh tit, or a redshank and a spotted redshank in winter plumage, or even a common buzzard (those which breed round here) and a honey buzzard (a few of which pass through as passage migrants) to see how minute the differences can be. And if you are in a race you have no time to consult your guidebook or hang around hoping for a better view in a few minute's time.

The SOS Spring Newsletter goes on to give an account of some of the more unusual birds seen during this year's Bird Race as well as during November, December and January. This is a period which included some of the coldest weather for forty years and a recurring theme is the disruption to distribution and behaviour amongst birds which this caused. Some local oddities included hen harriers at Pulborough Brooks and a snow bunting at Beeding. This latter would be rare anywhere but specially so that far inland and brings back memories that one was thought to have been seen the previous winter here on Fittleworth Common. There was also the amazing sight of a white-tailed eagle just down the road at Amberley Wild Brooks where there was also a flock of some 100 white-front geese. And, talking of geese, the Egyptian geese which have been a feature of Petworth Park lake for the past few years have multiplied and spilled over onto other near-by waters. Meanwhile the Canada geese which are a permanent feature of Petworth Park have been joined by greylags and, the other day there was the added excitement of a stray barnacle goose.

Wintering bitterns were plentiful across many wetland locations in the south with three long-stay birds at Burton Mill Lake. These brown, heron-like birds probably come in from Holland and will almost certainly return there to breed. If not, local residents will be entertained during the spring by the loud plangent booming of the males which goes on round the clock during spring and can be heard at least a mile away. Bitterns are also well-known for their ability to stand motionless and upright amongst reeds so that the markings on their breasts are a perfect camouflage. If the wind blows and the reeds bend they sway in unison.

Waxwings, which arrived in the north east in November had spread into Sussex and by January were cropping up in record numbers. Amongst many sightings were flocks of up to 40 birds each in Billingshurst, Rackham and Chichester; anywhere, in fact, where there were still berries. But perhaps the most extraordinary item of news comes via the BOT Garden Birdwatch wherein a participant from Hastings notes the appearance in his garden of no less than 180 goldfinches.

During the ten days preceding the filing for these notes we have enjoyed superb spring weather which has suddenly brought the countryside to life. The wild daffodils, always a spring treat, are having a particularly good year and so are the early butterflies. Bright yellow brimstones which have spent the winter tucked in out of sight amongst ivy leaves were out and about in early March and by early April the first of the season's hatchers, orange tips, were everywhere. But perhaps the biggest surprise was a photograph, taken locally in mid-April, of a writhing heap of a dozen or so grass snakes. Whatever they were up to, such behaviour is extremely rare. The photo can be seen at www. Sussex butterfly conservation/sightings. and is well worth a look.

May 2011

Collectors become conservationists

Such is the emphasis today on the need to conserve our dwindling stock of wildlife that it is easy to forget that until quite recently the fashion was to make collections of just about everything, be it fossils, beetles, seashells or butterflies. These were displayed in beautiful mahogany cabinets which were themselves masterpieces of the cabinet-makers art. Butterfly collectors in particular were an especially eclectic lot. Mildly eccentric perhaps but eminently respectable, their numbers included the aristocracy, clergymen, senior soldiers and doctors. There was, for instance, a British General who wrote with a sensitivity, in stark contrast with the business on hand, of the butterflies which he encountered whilst driving the Germans back across France in the bitter final stages of the second world war. Reading his story I was, for some reason, reminded of the occasion when the newly-ordained David Sheppard (later to become the Bishop of Liverpool) preached at matins in Melbourne Cathedral and then sauntered down to the cricket ground, opened for England and put the Aussies to the sword with an immaculate century.

One famous butterfly collector in his day was the Reverend John Marcon who lived in retirement here in Sandy Lane just across the road from where we now live. He is remembered by one of his contemporaries as a tall clergyman and manic collector who would drive his motorcycle at great speed on his way to the various collecting grounds in the southern counties. The same source recalls that on one occasion just after the war he collided head-on with a Canadian army jeep and was apparently pronounced dead at the scene by three doctors, one of whom was a Harley Street specialist. Despite this and after many months in a coma, he made a miraculous recovery. He did, however, conclude that the incident was a message from on high telling him to give up collecting, which he did. But in old-age he decided that he had sufficiently atoned for his sins and so resumed with undiminished vigour.

John Marcon specialised in collecting those butterflies which showed some deviation from the norm. Called aberrations, they come about in a variety of ways. There are, for instance, those which result from two species interbreeding. These hybrids are extremely rare and the outcome is always sterile. Then there are those which hatch from a chrysalis which has been damaged by extremes of temperature. These are usually distinguished by a dusting of dark pigments and were unusually plentiful during the second half of last summer. Another form are gynandromorphs. These are the outcome of a mis-functioning of the mechanism which determines gender and results in a mix of male and female characteristics scattered through their bodies and wings. And lastly are those wherein the aberration is imbedded in the genes and is therefore passed from generation to generation. If the feature bestows an advantage in the battle to survive the aberrant form will, in time, replace the norm as is happening in the case of the peppered moth which is predominantly white but has a dark form. This latter replaced the normal white form during the industrial revolution in areas of countryside where vegetation had been darkened by pollution. When the pollution disappeared and the advantage in terms of camouflage disappeared the white form returned.

Any of these curiosities brought lustre to the collections of old and bestowed upon the proud owners bragging rights over all others. However it would be unfair to blame these collectors for the present parlous state of so much of our butterfly fauna. With few exceptions this situation has been brought about by changes in land use and the attendant destruction of butterfly habitat. So now the enthusiasm which drove yesterday's collectors is channelled into conservation which is, happily, beginning to show good results. And for those of us who wish to record the beauty of these intriguing insects the modern camera is a much better tool than the net and killing bottle ever was.

June 2011

Life in the slow lane

People go to Sark because there are no cars, peaceful countryside and, George hopes, to see the sea birds. George is the island's bird expert, has a boat and runs daily trips around the island to see what's about. Sadly we missed out because of strong winds but we did pass his cottage and saw on a board a list of what might be expected. This included cormorants, shags, oystercatchers, guillemots, gannets and puffins; perhaps a touch optimistic because the breeding colonies of both gannets and puffins are some way off on other islands and any sighting would have been confined to a stray bird well beyond its normal range. But so what !! Any boat trip round Sark would take you to some magical places, birds or no birds.

So instead of an outing with George we had a tour of the island in a horse-drawn carriage and thus met John and Mary. The plan was to meet up by the duck pond, a couple of hundred yards across the field behind where we were staying. The duck pond turned out to be just that; a pond inhabited by mallard, the young already fully grown and fledged except for their primaries and this was a reminder that, although we, in late May, were wrapped up against a sharp east wind, an early spring had brought things forward. Then John and Mary came down the lane. We had already seen several carriages driven by ladies of style who would not have been out of place at a pony and trap event on the lawns of Windsor Park. John, on the other hand, resembled a pantomime pirate complete with a shaggy beard and hair to match. But beneath all this lay a placid, gentle, warm-hearted man entirely at one with the peaceful lanes along which he and Mary were to take us. We learnt that he came from Durham, spends the summer on Sark and the winter at Moidart up on the west coast of Scotland where he is a gamekeeper. He would be leaving Sark in time for the grouse shooting and told us that, in his other life he saw his role as custodian of a countryside in which there is room for all birdlife, including species of which other keepers might wish to be rid.

Mary, a five-year old, was bought from a Tyneside dealer and, John reckons, has another dozen years work in her. In hot weather John takes her down to the sea for a cooling dip before turning in. Mary seemed to us content with her lot but apparently can sulk if she feels that John is neglecting her in favour of his passengers. Our journey with them provided the opportunity to see from across the bay the stack upon which were the nesting guillemots, which are a high point in George's tour. It rose sheer out of the sea with narrow ledges where some 500 birds live out the full panoply of family life. Females lay just one egg each straight onto bare rock wherever they can find space. Eggs are pointed to ensure that, if knocked, they role in a tight circle and don't fall over the edge whilst chicks reach the sea by a process of tumbling, flapping and parental assistance. Once in the water parents continue to tend and feed them.

Guernsey allows cars but even so offers peaceful and varied countryside. To the north-west lie flat wide bays backed by extensive sand dunes whilst the south-east consists of high cliffs interspersed with small coves. And wherever you go the hedge-rows are festooned with honeysuckle and fields carpeted with thrift, bluebells, trefoils, ramsons, scabious and wild saxifrage. For those with an eye for butterflies a particular pleasure was to see so many wall browns, common in England 25 years ago but now in serious decline. But the high point for me was a surprise encounter with a strong little colony of Glanville fritillaries. My previous meeting with these butterflies had required a planned visit to the undercliffs along the south coast of the Isle of Wight which is the only place in Britain where they live. So to come across these exquisite rarities unexpectedly was a treat indeed.

And now back home to a garden and countryside prematurely robbed of the freshness of early summer by drought and drying winds. Two bits of contrasting news greet us. The first is from Christine Parker who found that a great spotted woodpecker had bored holes in either side of her nest-box and removed the entire clutch of baby blue tits from within. And from Sue Kitchener a happier story; she has a family of goldfinches as regular visitors to the feeders in her garden on the Fleet. Interestingly, they feed quite happily not just from nyger seed but peanuts as well.

July 2011

The extended family of wasps

To most of us a wasp is just a wasp; something which turns up when least wanted, is easily moved to anger and has a nasty sting. But to entomologists it is *vespula vulgaris* or common wasp, one of 8 species of social wasp in a family which, in this country alone, also contains 230 solitary wasps and innumerable parasitic wasps. Solitary wasps are loners so are less often seen. Indeed few even have an English name and those that do, have one which reflects the way they behave. Thus the potter wasp is so-called because it builds a neat little flask-shaped nest out of mud and saliva; mason wasps build theirs from sand or crumbling mortar and spider-hunting wasps catch spiders, sting them and then drag them, paralysed, down into their burrows where, still living, they are devoured by the wasp's larvae. And just in case the effect of the sting should wear off before the spider is eaten, the wasp forestalls escape by rather sweetly biting its legs off.

Parasitic wasps are so called because they insert their eggs into the living tissue of hosts which the hatching larvae then eat from within. Gall wasps parasitize plant tissue and ichneumons use animal tissue. Both are characterised by females which have adapted their organs of sting into needle-like projections from their rear-end called ovipositors. These they use to inject eggs into the host tissue. In some species these ovipositors can be as long again as their bodies and this makes them look pretty frightening. But in fact they are stingless and harmless to all but their hosts. A few months ago I came across one of the more fearsome-looking ichneumons, *Rhysella approximator* (sorry, it has no English name) working along the surface of a rotting log in Petworth Park. It had an inch-long black body with an ovipositor the same length again, long red legs and black antennae with which it was tapping the surface of the log. It was looking for the maggots of alder wasps which live in tunnels made in the fallen timber. I did not have long to wait for the action to start; almost immediately the insect reared up on its legs and with abdomen pointing skywards plunged its ovipositor vertically down ¾ inch through the wood slap into the maggot below. It was as if its whole being had been designed for this one act. And it gets nastier still because often there are other *Rhysella* standing by to use the same hole to lay their eggs and when all these hatch inside the doomed maggot the most robust larva eats the others before starting on its host.

This it does by first devouring those bits of the maggot that will not prove fatal, thereby retaining a supply of fresh food for as long as possible. But if all this sounds a bit gruesome there is comfort to be had from knowing that the simplicity of the grub's nervous system ensures that it is unaware of all the awful things going on inside it.

Vespula vulgans (the common wasp that spooks us when we have a picnic in summer) is by far the most common social wasp. It lives in nests which are made from chewed-up wood mixed with saliva to form a sort of papier mache and the result is a structure which is both complex and beautiful. The nest-building is started by the queen with a thing the size of a golf-ball within which are chambers into each of which she lays an egg. These hatch into grubs which become sterile worker wasps. The queen meanwhile continues to lay eggs whilst the workers feed the new young, enlarging the nest to accommodate the growing colony and defending it against intruders. By the end the nest is the size of a football and houses perhaps 2000 wasps. Towards the end of the summer males and females are produced which leave the nest to mate with those from other colonies. At this time the workers, their task now complete, also leave the nest and it is this general exodus which accounts for the huge increase in the number of wasps on the wing in late summer. As winter approaches all, except fertilised females, die off leaving the females to hibernate and emerge as next year's queens.

In the 1990's the numbers of our social wasps were swelled by the arrival from the continent of a slightly larger species called medians, an event which the newspapers sought to sensationalise by reporting that "a killer wasp from France" had arrived. In the event, however, median wasps settled peacefully amongst us and cause less trouble than our own native wasps. Which leaves just hornets, the largest and most handsome of all the social wasps. They have become more common recently and because of their size are given a wide berth by us humans. But actually they are extremely docile and will only sting (painfully it must be admitted) if unreasonably provoked. So admire them for what they are – large and impressive insects, but they don't like being prodded or sat upon.

August 2011

The quest for purple emperors

Greatly prized for their rarity and beauty, purple emperors have earned a special place in the pantheon of British butterflies. They fly throughout most of July and their elusive habits ensure that even in woods where they are known to exist they are seldom seen. This is because they spend most of the day in the tree tops, the males fighting each other for the most favourable perch from which to watch out for mates. As a consequence many people who go in search of these butterflies have to settle for nothing better than a glimpse through binoculars of two males in aerial battle high above the tree canopy. However, as with all butterflies, male purple emperors need certain salts to fuel up for the manly duties which lie ahead and these they acquire by drinking from puddles. Places enriched by animal waste such as the wet areas around cattle troughs are special favourites. These descents usually occur in the morning and offer a good opportunity to see them close up.

These singular habits have spawned a cult amongst butterfly enthusiasts keen to take advantage of such depraved tastes by concocting their own attractants, often with faintly ridiculous results. For example a couple of years ago a group of otherwise perfectly sane people, intent on finding which formulation was the most effective, set up in a woodland glade five breakfast tables complete with white cloths upon which were placed a selection of baits which included Pimms, Korean shrimp paste and horse manure (see www.purpleempire.com if you don't believe me). Bridget and I recently came across similar goings-on whilst walking in Botany Bay, a good spot for purple emperors between Dunsfold and Chiddingfold. By chance we had met up with another couple and as the four of us strolled along chatting and enjoying the company of different woodland butterflies there came into view a group of people sitting in the shade by the side of the track, cameras and binoculars at the ready, their attention focussed upon a small pile of something which had been placed in the middle of the path in front of them. As we approached there was a stir and whispers went round that a purple emperor had just settled on this heap, whereupon one of the group dropped to the ground and, in the manner of a lizard stalking a fly, edged forward to take a photo. But inevitably his movement disturbed the butterfly which took off like a startled snipe, and that was that. We heard later that this vigil had been going on for several hours and that this had been their first purple emperor sighting. Several had spent the previous day there with similar results. Others had brought picnics and, despite the poor return, everyone seemed to have enjoyed themselves. The one who had frightened the butterfly away was proud to tell us that the recipe used to create the nasty little pile around which they were gathered was age-ripened tuna mixed with something provided by his cat.

For butterflies in general it has been a mixed summer. An early spring brought out those which had hibernated as adults so that April gave us a good showing of brimstones and tortoiseshells. These were followed by newly-hatched orange tips and holly blues, the latter seeming to have benefited from recent severe winters which may have reduced the number of parasitic wasps which lay eggs in their caterpillars. Next came a couple of cool months without rain. The countryside dried up, wild flowers suffered and, with few exceptions, butterflies were scarce. Ones which did do well, however, were the silver studded blues on Iping Common just west of Midhurst. These delicate little butterflies, which have a symbiotic relation with ants much the same as the more celebrated large blues, inhabit heather-clad heathland which withstands drought better than most.

Rain in July brought the countryside back to life. Wild flowers bloomed and a pyramidal orchid appeared out of the blue on some rough ground in our garden. These pretty flowers are fairly plentiful on the calcareous soil up on the downs but here they are a great surprise. July sunshine has continued intermittently into August and those with bird tables have seen young birds, now fully-grown, still begging their parents for food. Both green and great spotted woodpeckers have been plentiful in village gardens and overhead families of buzzards have been circling around making cat-like noises whilst trying to dodge rooks. Swifts have already departed for Africa and, another sign of changing seasons, a green sandpiper passed through Petworth Park lake in July. Robins have re-acquired their red breasts after moulting and are already squabbling over winter territories. Flocks of crossbills are moving around but our chances of seeing them locally have been reduced by the recent felling of conifers on Coates Common. Nightjars have been heard churring at sundown around the village and should still be with us well into September.

September 2011

An enchanted Hampshire Down

For those whose vision of heaven includes wide expanses of uncultivated chalk downland, a good preview can be had by visiting Stockbridge Down. Bordered by the B3049 from Winchester to Stockbridge, there are two car parks about two miles before reaching Stockbridge town. The Down itself is hidden from view by a high hedge but all you have to do is go through a gate leading from either car park and there you are, with an uninterrupted access to 165 acres of ancient chalk downland. We were there in August and with all the mid-summer rain the flowers were at their best. Carpets of marjoram were interspersed with horseshoe vetch, harebells, scabious, round-headed rampion, wild mint and thyme. Thistles and various different knapweeds added shades of red and amongst them all stood tall clumps of hemp agrimony, their lavender-coloured flowers providing nectar for a whole host of different insects. And just to complete the scene were clumps of bushes, all laden with berries.

The Down is owned by the National Trust and managed by them in conjunction with English Nature. In truth, though, the only evidence of active management were signs that cattle had been in there earlier in the year. If so, one must suppose that this was part of a programme to ensure that invasive grasses would be grazed out and thereby prevented from overwhelming the flowers; good to see because the alarming fact is that in the space of the last seventy years a massive 98% of the flower-rich meadows in this country have been destroyed. The significance of this tragedy goes well beyond just the aesthetic degradation of our countryside and resides in the fact that, because plants capture energy from the sun, all life on land directly or indirectly depends upon them. Insects are an important part of this chain as well because their dependence upon flowers for nectar ensures that in the process of feeding they act as pollinators and without them plant-life would quickly die out. The most frequently mentioned pollinators are honeybees and it is said that they alone are involved in one way or another in the production of a third of all the food we eat. Albert Einstein put it this way; if bees disappeared, within four years there would be no food left for us humans to eat.

Honeybees are, of course, not the only pollinators. Butterflies, moths, hover flies, bumblebees and ants all play a significant part as well and Stockbridge Down is alive with them all; The NT say that thirty species of butterfly breed on the Down which is impressive when you realise that each requires its own mini-habitat. Our visit in mid-August coincided with the high point in the flight period of chalkhill blues. These are one of several species of downland butterflies which were badly hit when the rabbit population was decimated by myxamitosis leaving coarse grass to grow up and smother the plants upon which their caterpillars feed. So it was nice to see them back in such good numbers. The males are a milky blue and have a way of fluttering just above the grass looking for the chocolate brown females perched demurely below. To be there on a sunny summer day is to see butterflies and wild flowers as nature intended, in perfect harmony one with the other.

In such a place any old butterfly flying around is going to look good but if one suddenly turns up which is so rare that only a few years ago it was on the verge of extinction, then that's something very special. And this was exactly what happened that day when we came across a small colony of silver spotted skippers. About twice the size of a house-fly, with bright golden-brown wings, large puppy-like eyes and furry bodies, they only fly when the air temperature is above 20°C and then dart about close to the ground. When later I showed a friend some photos I'd taken she said that if she had seen one she would have taken it for a moth. No surprise really because for some reason skippers have retained many of the primitive anatomical features which were common to all lepidoptera before butterflies and moths evolved into separate groups. Skippers are day-fliers but then so are some moths. They have butterfly-like clubbed antennae and perch, uniquely, with their hindwings flat and forewings pointing slightly upwards. Actually there is no one single anatomical feature which on its own separates butterflies from moths, a fact which reminds us that all living things evolved in a random fashion in response to the conditions with which they were faced and not according to some neat pre-ordained blueprint. Taxonomists have been left to classify them into groups to facilitate scientific study and this can sometimes leave room for doubt.

October 2011

Nature Matters

The waterfowl of Petworth Park

A walk round the lakes in Petworth Park provides a good opportunity to see three species of geese, albeit ones which owe their presence here to ancestors first brought to this country to add lustre to ornamental collections from which they later escaped or were farmed. The most prominent of these are Canada geese which arrived here in the late seventeenth century to be added to the royal collection in St James's Park. Easily recognised by their large size, black heads and necks and white cheeks, feral birds quickly spread through the country and now they are probably the one goose to which most people can put a name. Around here they fly and graze all along the Rother and sometimes nest in the water-meadows just along from the bridge. Another species which started its life in this country as part the royal collection is the Egyptian goose. These strange-looking tree-nesting birds, more closely related to shelducks than geese, were prized additions to collections everywhere and escapees began to spread so widely that by the 1970s they too were added to the list of native British wild birds. The first sighting on the lakes at Petworth was about ten years ago since when numbers have increased so that this year at least five separate families were raised successfully.

More recently these two have been joined by greylag geese, a species which is widely distributed throughout Eurasia. In this country it is represented by a race which is descended from the domestic geese which were farmed in East Anglia in the nineteenth century for meat as well as plumes which before the advent of steel nibs, were used for writing. They are thought to have come originally from Egypt and in all probability our present greylags are the result of them having interbred with our native wild birds the numbers of which are greatly increased in winter by the arrival of some 80,000 migrants from Iceland. Although small flocks have been around here for some time they are relatively new to Petworth Park Lakes and the sight of perhaps a couple of hundred there in mid-September was a surprise.

An unusual pair of ducks which I saw there recently turned out to be paradise shelducks, natives of New Zealand. Larger than a mallard, the duck has a chestnut body, white head and neck and blue beak and legs and the drake a black head and dark body. Oddly enough I remember seeing a pair there during the cold weather of last winter and thought nothing of it. But now that they have re-appeared I have had second thoughts; they pair for life, these duck, and the idea that they might have been captive birds which have eloped and raised a family somewhere in the wild is not without a certain romance.

Whilst it is true to say that Petworth wildfowl could never match the spectacle of several hundred pink-foot coming in off the North Sea against a cold winter sunset, the park, with its beautiful rolling vistas and quiet corners where wildlife can flourish unmolested by human traffic, has a charm of its own and should not be dismissed. Other waterfowl which I have seen on the lakes which are beyond all argument native, are the ubiquitous mallard, tufted duck, shoveller, shelduck, coot, moorhen, great-crested grebe, and black-headed gull; also green sandpipers, an unusual visitor which sometimes turns up on passage. About the size of a snipe but with a white rump, it flies in typical sandpiper fashion with rapid wing-beats interspersed with glides. They pass through the south of England on the way to and from their breeding grounds in the tundra and their timetable is so erratic that it is sometimes hard to know whether they are coming or going.

Our visits to the park are random and not solely to see the birds, so this list is far from comprehensive. Other water birds must come and go and it would be a surprise if pintail, gadwell and perhaps even goldeneye didn't show up in winter. And I have not included the brief visit last winter of a single barnacle goose, a bird which breeds in Greenland or Spitsbergen and comes to the Hebrides and the Solway for the winter. It seems that the odd bird sometimes mistakenly joins the flock of a different species migrating through its territory and as a consequence ends up in the wrong place and I once before saw a barnacle grazing amongst brents at Pagham. But how one barnacle on its own could find itself in amongst a largely sedentary and isolated group like the Petworth Park lot goodness alone knows.

November 2011

Greylag

Egyptian goose

Wildlife along the Arun valley

The many springs and streams which flow from the high weald and surrounding downs into the coastal plains ensure that Sussex is particularly rich in wetland. Although in recent years many of the natural characteristics which were so beneficial to wildlife, have been damaged by changes in land use, there are exceptions. One such is the area through which the Arun runs between Pulborough and Amberley. Here the river has been allowed, in winter, to flood over the surrounding plains thereby creating ideal conditions for marsh plants, birds and invertebrates, a situation which has been safeguarded and enhanced by the concerted action of the RSPB at Wiggonholt and the Sussex Wildlife Trust (SWT) at Amberley Brooks and Waltham Marsh.

The first thing RSPB did before opening the Wiggonholt reserve in 1991 was to install systems to control the depth of water at levels which met the needs of the various water-birds which were already there; deep water for divers, shallow for up-enders and dabblers, damp meadows for the grazers and so on. Marshland which had been grazed sporadically without regard to nesting birds was brought under control and reed-beds were encouraged. Thus was created a range of habitats which has increased numbers and encouraged nesting. So well has the plan worked that Wiggonholt has not only become the Society's flagship reserve in the south east but is also designated a place of international importance for wintering wildfowl. Encouraged by these successes the reserve has recently been extended to include woodland and heath, thereby increasing the range of birds and indeed other wildlife present there. For example by the sympathetic management of blackthorn, Wiggonholt has become one of the few places hereabouts where the rare and elusive brown hairstreak butterfly breeds.

As with any place where naturalists gather, there is a constant stream of well-informed observers on hand to spot and identify anything which turns up. Thus the list of sightings, posted each day on a board at the entrance to the reserve, includes (according to season) such rarities as cranes, bitterns, spoonbills, garganey, Bewick's swans, wood sandpipers, ruffs, white-fronted geese, short-eared owls, peregrines, lesser spotted woodpeckers and merlins. Add to these, in winter, the huge flocks of teal, wigeon and lapwing grazing in the water-meadows and its easy to see the attractions.

Just to the south of Wiggonholt further down the valley lies the Waltham Brooks reserve which consists of a large area of open water and grazing marshes either side of the river. A car-park just to the west of Greatham bridge provides access to footpaths either along the river or across the bridge, through to Amberley Wildbrooks. There is also a path which is rather rough going, which follows the course of the now disused Wey and Arun Navigation canal. In winter teal, pintail, pochard, shoveller, gadwell and mallard are guaranteed with the possibility of redshank and snipe. In times of migration whimbrel and green sandpipers sometimes show and in winter short eared owls hunt over the meadows. Although the reserve was purchased by the SWT in 1984 the Trust has only recently acquired the grazing rights. As a result future grazing will be managed for the benefit of ground-nesting birds and flowers.

To the south of Waltham Brooks lies Amberley Wildbrooks, the one running seamlessly into the other. Much of the Wildbrooks is low-value farmland and SWT work closely with owners to ensure that the interests of all parties are safeguarded. Thus, by working in partnership with the RSPB, there is now a continuous high-quality, well managed wetland stretching all the way from Pulborough to the foot of the downs. The benefits from such large-scale integrated conservation which takes account of the needs of all forms of wildlife as well as of other land users are immense.

One of the nice things about a place like this is that you never know what's just round the corner. I remember a few years ago early in January walking from Greatham bridge through to the Amberley Wildbrooks. It was a beautiful sunny day, frost in the air and a sprinkling of over-night snow on the ground. The countryside, against the backdrop of the downs was at its sparkling best. In no particular order we had for company a woodcock, several flocks of meadow pipets, a small herd of roe deer, grazing Bewick's swans, a marsh harrier and a battleship-grey male hen harrier; and to cap it all, a party of goosanders grateful to have found some unfrozen water along the river. On a similar walk at a different time of year we could have been amongst nightingales, grasshopper warblers, nightjars and skylarks; we might have watched courting lapwings performing their strange aerial tumbles and heard snipe drumming. We would certainly have seen a few of the rarer British dragonflies. And all this in a place which boasts something like half of all the water plant species native to this country.

All this here, right on our doorstep.

December 2011

Antarctica; a Centenary to remember

On 14th June 1910 a team of explorers sailed from Cardiff on the *s.s. Terra Nova* bound for Antarctica and on to the South Pole. Seven months later a base camp had been established at McMurdo Sound and the first major sledging party was heading south. About a year later, on the 17th January 1912, the five who made the final assault were standing on the Pole. The expedition leader was Captain Robert Scott and the doctor and chief of scientific staff was Edward Wilson. The others were Evans, Oates and Bowers. Only 40, Wilson had already established a reputation as a wildlife artist of the same rank as Millais and Thorburn and had spent the early stages on board ship completing a definitive work on grouse disease. All had had previous experience of the Antarctic but had never experienced conditions as bad as those encountered in the final stages at sea.. Now before them lay a trek over ice, glaciers and an ice-cap which was to take just over a year.

Their priority was scientific research, an objective from which they never wavered despite the additional burdens this imposed. Amongst Wilson's tasks was to test an idea that Emperor Penguins might provide the missing evolutionary link between birds and dinosaurs. Science had already shown that embryonic development frequently retraces certain aspects of an animal's evolutionary history, so he collected eggs at different stages of incubation. From these he extracted the chicks and preserved them for later dissection, all of which cost several extra days. Likewise his geological specimens added weight to his sledge but included a fossilized leaf which resembled that of a beech tree, a discovery which shed new light on the state of our planet's past climate. Wilson could often to be found late at night in his tent working on his specimens or finishing his paintings, standing, the better to stay awake. This, on top of his work as doctor, dog-team leader and confidante to Scott, set the standards of commitment and endurance which pervaded the whole team.

The five chosen to make the final assault on the pole knew that a team from Norway, led by Roald Amundsen was also on its way and that Amundsen had just one simple aim; to be the first there. Scott, on the other hand, was never prepared to compromise his team's scientific work in the interest of speed. Even so there can be little doubt that the English, too, hoped to be the first, an aim sharpened by the fact that just two years earlier another British attempt on the Pole lead by Ernest Shackleton had failed by a mere 51 miles. Imagine, then, their feelings when they approached their goal only to find a Norwegian flag flying from a pole plonked on a heap of snow surrounded by fresh sledge tracks. It mattered little that their own readings showed that the Norwegians were some three miles adrift; Scott conceded that Amundsen had beaten them by just a few days. There is said to be a wonderful photograph of him standing there taking it all in whilst quietly smoking a cigarette. It would be another fifty years before the next person set foot on the South Pole.

So now they must turn their minds to the return journey. Wilson's diaries speak of men with severely frost-bitten cheeks, noses and hands. He himself was suffering from snow-blindness though he told no-one. And worst of all there lay before them a climb of 1000 feet and Evans was weakening. They were thousands of miles from the nearest human habitation and communication with the outside world was impossible. These men were tough in mind and body but would have been aware of the odds against them. On 17th February Evans, still working his sledge, died of fatigue. Shortly after Titus Oates, feet so badly frost-bitten that he could scarcely walk and fearful that he was impeding the other three, left the tent one night with words which have passed into the lexicon of famous sayings; "I'm just going outside and may be gone some time". The temperature outside was 40° below and he was never seen again. Scott, Wilson and Bowers pressed on but it was no good; on 11th March they perished as they lay in their tent, frozen and preserved in death where they were found eight months later by a search party. They were just 11 miles short of relief supplies deposited on the way out.

The search party also recovered their scientific specimens, diaries and Wilson's sketch books as well as the last letters to their families written from that tent by the beleaguered men. There was no self-pity, only the matter-of-fact reporting of matters pertaining to the trip. Captain Scott's letter to his wife included the wish that she "make the boy interested in Natural History: it's better than games. They teach it at some schools". The boy was of course his son, the three-year-old Peter who grew up to be a bronze medallist in sailing at the 1936 Olympics, British National Gliding Champion in 1963 but above all founder of the Wildfowl And Wetland Trust and a wildlife conservationist and artist of international repute. And finally there was Edward Wilson. Scott's diaries and the writings of others who chronicled the expedition speak of a man who never tired of tending the needs of others and who led by personal example. His contribution to the understanding of the natural history of Antarctica was profound and his superb paintings of landscape and fauna, executed often with numbed hands by the light of a hurricane lamp, served to show the world a beauty which, 100 years later, we still marvel at on television from the comfort of our armchairs. But it is only by reading the more intimate passages from his own diaries that we learn that this remarkable man was sustained by an unbreakable faith, so strong that he went daily into the crow's nest on the *Terra Nova* for private prayer. At such times, he tells us, the thought of his wife, at home in England, was so strong that he felt her presence was there by his side as they, together, confronted the fierce storms and everlasting wilderness of Antarctica.

January 2012

What makes plants grow and birds sing?

Imagine that you have the cutting of a carnation sitting in a small pot on your windowsill. After several weeks, with a little luck, you should have a nice bushy plant with several buds ready to plant out in the garden. But you are sure to have noticed that the amount of soil in the pot is still the same as when you first planted the cutting.. So why is the plant now so much larger when all you have added is a little water? After all an animal needs to eat regular quantities of solid, bulky food to grow and stay alive, so why not plants? This is a question which bothered botanists of old who had already observed several other interesting things about plants. First, their experiments had shown that if they put the young plant in the dark it grew fast and floppy, the leaves turned yellow and eventually it died. Next, if they placed the young plant in a fridge, again it died. From this they concluded that a green plant, if it is to grow and thrive, must have three things; daylight, warmth and of course the water which enables it to absorb nutrients in the soil through their roots.

But there was still something missing and the puzzle was not solved until laboratory experiments demonstrated that plants also need carbon dioxide, a gas which is naturally present in the Earth's atmosphere and which all living things, plants and animals, expire but which plants also absorb through microscopic holes in their leaves and stems called stomata. In the presence of sunlight plants produce chlorophyll within their cells. This makes them look green and enables the carbon dioxide and water in the leaf to combine in a chemical reaction which results in sugars being formed and oxygen to be excreted as a waste product. This chemical reaction is called photosynthesis and the sugars that are thereby formed are changed by the plant into other carbohydrates such as starch. The addition of other elements from the soil result in the creation of proteins and fats and it is this which enables plants to grow healthily without the need to ingest bulky foods as do animals. Plants kept in the dark such as forced rhubarb grow without developing chlorophyll, there is no photosynthesis and growth results from cells elongating. The plant becomes long and spindly; nice and tender for eating but physically weak.

All this highlights something which is essential for the maintenance of a healthy life on earth, namely that whilst animals take in oxygen and excrete carbon dioxide plants also soak up carbon dioxide. Each, therefore, assists the other, something which has come about as the two major life-forms have evolved side by side over hundreds of millions of years. Anything which disturbs this balance is a major threat to both. Thus the importance of the rain forests of Brazil and Asia over which the Earth's atmosphere is circulated by wind currents and enables them to act as factories which re-oxygenate the air all animals breathe and at the same time remove the carbon dioxide which is a major component of greenhouse gas.

Now for some thoughts about what makes birds sing, something which seems appropriate as we approach spring. First, though, we should bear in mind what the experts say, which is that all bird behaviour is motivated by one of just three basic instincts. These are feeding, breeding and self-defence. So which of these prompts song? The answer is probably a bit of all three according to circumstances. Thus a winter flock of, say, chaffinches moving through a beech wood keep up an incessant chirping to help keep together and by keeping together they stand a better chance than would an individual of both finding food and spotting potential danger. The bird world is replete with such examples. As for breeding, it is well-known that with song-birds only males sing and this is mostly confined to the breeding season. It is therefore easy to assume that this is simply a device to attract a mate. But if this were so, why do male migrants start to sing immediately upon arrival in their breeding quarters even though the females wont arrive for at least another week? And why, having found a mate and started a family, do the males give themselves over to a life of polygamy? People who study these things tell us the answer is that male song is as much to do with territorial defence as with courtship, which comes as a disappointment to those of us who naively believe that a singing skylark is serenading his beloved to soothe her as she dutifully incubates their eggs whereas, in truth, he is just as likely to be picking a fight with the neighbours.. Which leaves just self-defence and here we have to stretch the definition of song to include the much less melodious alarm call with which, say, a. blackbird might announce the presence of a cat. Not all birds include these calls in their repertoire but those that do act as sentinels for everything else within range.

And finally news about the difficulties posed by unseasonably warm spells of winter weather which confront animals that try to hibernate. We have all seen bumble bees flying in December and red admiral butterflies fluttering around whatever blossom they can find whenever there is a shaft of winter sun. But nothing matches the young lizard which came into a house in The Gardens just before Christmas and nonchalantly plonked itself in the middle of the sitting room floor.

February 2012

A bird's eye view of Britain

Every spring about a hundred and twenty million land birds take up territories, build nests and raise young somewhere within the 57 million acres which make up the British Isles. Add to these the many millions of sea birds which come to our coastal cliffs and islands, plus those just passing through on their way elsewhere and we have a total list of some 595 different species. Of these roughly 51 come here in the spring just to breed and, having done so, return to their winter quarters. Their place is taken by about 48 other species which have spent the summer nesting far to the north of Britain and come here for the relative warmth of our winter. The rest, the residents, include some 100 species which are also found in neighbouring countries and 33 which are sufficiently different to be classed as sub-species. Occasionally one of their near-relatives turns up here and quickly draws a crowd, as happened recently when a Spanish sparrow found itself in a small village garden in Hampshire and pulled in so many twitchers that the locals made a killing selling them tea and cakes.

Even a few of our resident birds are represented by both nominate and sub-species. Thus it is that Irish jays and dippers are darker than those elsewhere in Britain and Irish coal tits have yellow, not white, cheeks. Also the islands of Shetland and Outer Hebrides each have their own distinctive wrens. It's all a bit like the the Galapogos Islands where, in 1836, Charles Darwin noticed that the same species of finch was represented on each island by a slightly different form. These variants he attributed to different feeding requirements, a conclusion which set in train his thesis on the origin of species.

The arrival of summer visitors each year lights up the countryside and tells us that spring has arrived. They come from places as far-off as southern Europe, Africa and, as with the arctic tern, Antarctica. These extraordinary little birds with their graceful flight migrate from one end of the planet to the other on wings too slender to take advantage of the energy-saving thermals which assist other long-distance travellers. It is reckoned that they spend about 9 months a year commuting. A few years ago some were joined in their north-bound Odyssey by an albatross which then lived happily amongst the sea birds in the Hebrides - happily, that is, until he fell in love with a gannet and, over-enthusiastic, was chucked out. Many migrants charm us by returning each year to exactly the same nesting place, a habit which results in couples which have not seen each other for more than half the year re-uniting in matrimony. Swallows and puffins are famous for this and the fact that science cannot yet explain precisely how this feat of navigation is achieved adds to the magic.

Nesting sea birds also have a charm of their own. Some have been roaming the seas all winter and only return to land to nest and others travel in as genuine migrants. Some, like guillemots, razorbills and kittiwakes gather into huge colonies, packed tight on narrow cliff-side ledges. Gannets, several thousand birds clustered together on one small stack jutting out of the sea, build nests so close that they touch. Puffins need places where there is enough earth to excavate the burrows in which they nest. And interspersed amongst these are the solitary nesters; fulmars, gulls, cormorants, shags, sea-duck, divers and grebes. All are specialist feeders and are critically dependent upon the right fish stock.. When summer is over all these visitors leave us and return to wherever they came from. Then with autumn come the geese, swans, duck and waders to spend the winter on our mudflats, tidal estuaries, and inland lakes. Flocks of redwings, fieldfares, bramblings and - if we're lucky - waxwings come in from Scandinavia to strip our shrubs of berries.

All birds share the same basic needs; a plentiful supply of food, a place to build a nest and raise a family and somewhere safe to live. Not all birds find all three in one place which lasts all year round and if they don't like where they are they can fly off elsewhere. Thus bird populations are constantly in flux. Usually such movements are in response to changing seasons, a situation complicated by recent unusually erratic climate. But a far larger problem is caused by the destruction of habitat which has come about over the past 50 years as a consequence of changes in land use. Not only have birds themselves been squeezed out but so have the things they eat. Set against this, however, is that over the same half century the number of species on the British list has actually increased by 170, a fact which undoubtedly says much about the huge growth in numbers of knowledgeable amateurs, equipped now with high-powered telescopes, often with built-in cameras which ensures that very little passes un-noticed and unrecognised. And the good news is that these birders regularly report their findings to a central electronic data base where trends are noted and conclusions used to guide conservation plans. As a consequence conservationists and other land users can now often work together to their mutual benefit. Amongst the beneficiaries, for example, have been red kites, ospreys, cranes, little egrets, avocets and black flycatchers, all birds which first came here of their own accord and then prospered from conservation. White-tailed eagles and bustards are two examples of birds which have been re-established in this country using entirely foreign stock. Others, of course, teeter on the edge of extinction but at least their welfare is now in the hands of those who understand their needs and care.

March 2012.

Nature Matters

Where have all the wild flowers gone?

A recent television series presented by Sarah Raven describes her crusade to encourage selected municipal authorities to include insect-friendly flowers when planting up their public spaces. Underpinning her proposition are three factors; first that over the past seventy years wild flowers in this country have declined by a massive 98%, second that without flowers to provide nectar for the insects which pollinate them, insects, along with many foods which are vital to us, would die out, and third that because most pollinating insects have evolved over tens of millions of years side by side with wild flowers, their mouth-parts are often unable to take nectar from the more recently introduced more colourful cultivars favoured for public parks. Simply put, pollination is the means by which the male pollen grains produced by the flower's stamen reaches the female part of the flower called the stigma. This is necessary to ensure fertilization. Pollen is spread in various ways; wind, birds and even bats all play a part. But by far the most usual is by visiting insects like bees, butterflies, moths and flies.

Large skipper feeding on clover

Whilst most flowers attract insects by providing nectar, in a competitive world this is often backed up by supplementary lures. Such a one is for the flower to pretend to be a prospective mate either by emitting a scent which mimics the pheromone which insects use to find each other, or by growing petals which make it look like the insect-mate itself. Either way the visitor gets a good coating of pollen which is then brushed off onto the next flower it visits and the job is done.

Relationships such as these have evolved over time and have resulted in instances where a particular species of insect and flower have become interdependent. This is well illustrated by a huge Madagascan hawk moth, the existence of which was predicted many years before it was actually found simply because there was known to be an orchid with a floral spur so long that it could only be pollinated by an insect with an equally long proboscis.

These and similar inter-relationships are found across all pollinating insects and flowers and is the main reason why butterfly populations in particular are so vulnerable to the destruction of wild flowers. Other insects have evolved life-styles which improve their efficiency as nectar-gatherers. Thus worker honey-bees returning to the hive indulge in elaborate dances and buzzings which tell the others both the direction and distance from the hive of newly-found nectar sources as well as their relative food value. Other examples are the beautiful little hover-flies which are constantly busy around flower-heads all summer; they themselves are stingless but they ensure themselves a safe passage by mimicking bees and wasps.

It is an important part of Sarah Raven's crusade to understand the reason for the catastrophic decline in wild flowers and here we can do no better than read the words of the aptly named Charles Flower who is pioneering practical methods of wild flower restoration on his own 175-acre farm in Wiltshire. In his book *"Where have all the flowers gone?"* he writes;

> "Our countryside used to be full of wild flowers. The hay meadows were particularly rich because the needs of the farmer so closely matched those of wildlife and flowers in particular. The mixed farm with its meadows, pastures and cornfields and its infrastructure of hedges, ponds, green paths and woods provided sufficient diversity of habitat for our wild flowers and attendant wildlife"

Charles Flower goes on to remind us that within nine years of Britain joining the Common Market in 1973 the price of corn jumped from £30 to £120 per ton with the result that farming was mechanised, hedgerows were torn up, woodland cleared, pesticides were used indiscriminately and there were generous grants for what he describes as the systematic destruction of our countryside. So this is the background against which Sarah Raven is campaigning and so far her considerable energy has been directed towards those who tend public flower-beds in inner cities. But a far bigger challenge awaits her when, as she must, she tries to get these same authorities to include in their planting the things necessary to sustain insects, specially butterflies, at other stages in their life-cycle. These include thistles, nettles, trefoils, vetches, grasses and so on; in other words things gardeners call weeds. And then, when all this is done, a way must be found to spread these pockets of inner city excellence out into the countryside where the problem started in the first place.

April 2012

Nature Matters

Spring butterflies

The first butterfly of the year is always a good thing to see and if it looks a bit bedraggled this is only to be expected. After all it's been around since the previous summer and has spent the intervening time asleep in some secluded hiding place where, with luck, it will have escaped being eaten by spiders. Several species hibernate like this, as adults; small tortoiseshells, peacocks, commas and brimstones are the most usual but are sometimes joined by red admirals which used to come here only as migrants but now seem to be able to survive our milder winters. Also there are speckled woods which have the unique ability to choose whether to hibernate either as adults or pupae. If the former they, too, will be flying in early spring. All these butterflies are big, strong insects, well able to store the large amounts of food necessary to live out the cold winter months. But even so if an early spell of warm weather brings them out of hibernation before nectar-bearing flowers have opened, they could find themselves unable to replace the energy they use up and so perish. One feature shared by all these species is that they have under-wing markings which provide perfect camouflage when the butterfly is at rest, wings folded above its head.

Unlike queen bumblebees which hibernate with their eggs already fertilized, hibernating butterflies wake up not only with their food reserves in urgent need of replenishment but also with the tedious job of finding a mate still requiring attention. This probably explains the air of desperation which often characterizes early spring butterflies. But it is important that they do things properly because it is their off-spring that will provide us with the hatchlings which decorate the countryside in the second half of summer.

All these butterflies are soon joined by those which have hatched from pupae and are immediately noticeable by a freshness and energy which perfectly matches the mood of spring. The first out are orange-tips. As with all butterflies the males hatch a few days before the females which have black rather than orange tips to their wings. The underside of both sexes are marked with delicate green marbling and this helps to distinguish them from the similar small whites which fly at the same time. Both are soon joined by large whites, and green-veined whites and the similarity between all of them has led to the creation of the shared name; cabbage whites. Consequently the belief has arisen that all are the enemy of vegetable growers. This is unfair because it's only the caterpillars of large whites which do anything like serious damage to brassica crops and even then only when our native population is swelled late in summer by immigrants from across the Channel. Amongst others which might turn up in May are migrant painted ladies. Remember these? They are the ones which came here in such vast numbers three years ago but have hardly been seen since. Small coppers can pop up anywhere and two little gems which can easily be overlooked are holly blues and green hairstreaks. If you see any blue butterfly flying around above head-height and settling on holly or ivy you can be sure that it's a pretty little holly blue and well worth a closer look. Also green hairstreaks which are less plentiful but widely distributed. The topside is dull brown and the underside is a soft shade of green which is unique amongst British butterflies. They are easy to approach and usually perch so that you can see their large black puppy-like eyes ringed by bands of black and white; hence its generic name, *Callophrys*, which is Greek for "beautiful eyebrow".

For other spring butterflies it is best to visit specialist habitats. Up on the downs there will be both small and common blues as well as duke of burgundies and various skippers (which, incidentally, the experts have now decided to classify as moths rather than butterflies, a change from which this column, wedded as it is to the habits of a lifetime, will claim exemption). Then in the woodland glades where volunteer workers have re-established the habitat that existed in the days when woodland was regularly coppiced you may find pearl-bordered fritillaries flitting amongst bugle. These may lack the grandeur of their mid-summer relatives but, with their opalescent markings and quiet elegance they hold their own in any company. I remember seeing them two a penny in the early 1950s along the railway cutting leading west from Fittleworth station but now we must go either to Oaken Wood north of Plaistow or Rewell Wood south-west of Arundel, to have any chance.

On, now, to other things; it's always nice to see an unusual bird in an unexpected place and so it was a couple of weeks ago when we stopped off at Coates Common to give Percy, our dog, a run. We took the path which runs back from the car park parallel with Coates Lane and there, a couple of hundred yards along, foraging in leaves under the oak trees was a male yellowhammer. No big deal really but with its bright yellow head and flanks tinged with chestnut, enough to remind me that I had not seen one for a very long time and never before in open woodland, and certainly enough to light up an otherwise rather hum-drum day.

May 2012

Nature Matters

A spring in two parts & a tragedy remembered

The poet Robert Browning may well have yearned to be in England now that April's there, but he had clearly overlooked the lot of birds which, encouraged by a warm and sunny March, had built nests and laid eggs only to find that, come April, they were sitting in sodden nests and a biting east wind which is precisely what has happened this year. Tree-nesters will have suffered little more than discomfort but not so the ground nesters, especially those which live beside water where they risk having their nests and eggs deluged by floods.

Despite the topsy-turvy weather, however, many of the summer visitors had arrived on schedule and by mid-April an osprey had returned to the same nest in Perthshire for the 25th consecutive year and laid its first egg. Five white storks, two glossy ibises and a rose-coloured starling were setting pulses racing along the coast between Selsey and Littlehampton and on 17th April a hobby was flying around on Coates Common. These small falcons are such superb fliers that they accompany migrating swallows, catching and eating them on the wing. Appropriate, then, that we saw the first swallows of the year the next day hunting insects over the main lake in Petworth Park. And talking of swallows reminds me that I recently read somewhere that there is now firm evidence that females, given a choice, always select as a mate the male with the longest tail. This news may cause Darwinians amongst us to conclude that swallows of the future will come to resemble tiny fast-flying peacocks.

Continuing our walk round Petworth Park lake that day the scene was dominated by the presence of an unusual number of Egyptian geese. First, one flew in and settled high up in a dead beech tree at the far end of the lake. I knew they were tree-nesters but even so to see a somewhat ungainly goose, webbed feet stretched out in front as if landing on water, alight on a branch with all the grace of a small perching bird seemed odd. As we continued our walk to the far side of the lake we came across about a dozen more grazing peacefully in rough grass and further off down by the water there was a mother with 12 new-born goslings. Then, to round things off, we came across a female keeping close guard over just one newly-hatched gosling and could only guess that the rest had fallen victim to the lake's voracious pike.

This sombre thought was repeated when 5 tiny mallard chicks came bustling along the edge of the water with no parents anywhere in sight. What on earth could have happened to make orphans of ones so young; and more important what now were their chances of survival? This question brought back a childhood memory of when I had joined forces with a broody hen to act as a foster-parent to a clutch of 13 mallard eggs. The situation had arisen when I visited a nest which I had had under observation for a couple of weeks only to find it abandoned and nearby all the signs of a fox-kill. Luckily, though, the eggs were undamaged and, even more fortunate, I knew that back at the farm where we lived there was a broody hen sitting on china eggs. So, using my pullover as a carrier, I gathered them up, ran back to the farm and slipped them in under her.

To start with things went well and within 24 hours all but one of the mallard eggs had hatched and the chicken had apparently not rumbled the unusual appearance of her family. As for me, I made the seemingly sensible decision that if they were ducks they should have water. So I dug a hole deep enough to take a spare cattle trough which was lying around, filled it with water and sat back to watch. It was then that the problems started; after a day or so swimming around my ducklings began to keel over and, without any obvious reason, expire. In desperation I rang up a local game-farm and was told that, until they grow their own feathers, ducklings are water-proofed by contact with the oily feathers of their mothers. Without this contact their down becomes waterlogged and their tiny bodies fatally chilled. Land-birds such as chickens do not have oily feathers and this was the problem. Was this, then, to be the fate of the motherless ducklings we had just seen in Petworth Park?

Had I known all this 24 hours earlier I could have removed the water and saved half the brood. As it was just one survived and she only after extensive bed-rest complete with a hot-water bottle and the odd shot of dilute cognac filched from my father and dispensed with an eye dropper. For the next year she lived with the chickens and once fledged had access to a pond. During the school holidays she followed me round and fed from my hand and after a while my pocket money stretched to the cost of a drake, bought from the game-farm whose advice had, earlier, saved her life. The next spring the two raised a family and, with the coming of autumn, all of them flew off into the wild where they belonged.

June 2012

Nature Matters

The charm of sea-birds

The phone call came out of the blue. It was from a friend to say that he and his wife had been offered places on a converted lifeboat leaving Milford Haven on the coming Sunday. The purpose was to visit an uninhabited 11-acre volcanic rock 10 miles off the coast of Pembroke called Grassholm. The attraction was that 35,000 gannets nest there each year and as his wife didn't fancy the idea would I come instead? And so it was that I found myself one June morning standing on the quayside in Milford Haven gazing into an impenetrable sea mist. Our party consisted of our leader and owner of the boat who was head of the local Field Studies Centre, 2 big shots from the RSPB and the two of us. Our leader's assessment of the situation was simple; it would be mad, he reckoned, to set out in such conditions but as we had all travelled so far to get there he was prepared to give it a go. The boat, after all, was equipped with a compass and a map, our destination lay 11 miles due west and he had a watch. What more did we need? In any case if we kept down-wind we could pick up the scent of decayed seaweed, rotting fish and droppings which is an inseparable part of an active gannetry.

So off we went and after a while the smell told us that we were on course. And then as if by a miracle; the sun broke through, the mist cleared and there just in front of us was this huge rock rising out of the sea and all around us were thousands of these great cigar-shaped birds with their scythe-like wings which span 6-foot wheeling around and diving into the sea after fish. We dropped anchor 20 yards off the rock and went ashore by rubber dingy. A steep climb led up to where the gannets had worn away a 2-acre patch to bear rock where they built their nests. The advice from our RSPB companions was that if we sat no nearer than 20 yards from the edge of the colony the birds would ignore us. They themselves had work to do which would take about three hours.

When not breeding gannets roam the sea. For the most part they mate for life and their first task upon returning to their colonies is to re-constitute their nests with seaweed. In due course a single egg is laid and from that moment onwards one of the pair is always present either to incubate or keep guard. Nests are closely packed but just far enough apart to avoid violent stabs from irritated neighbours. Even so powerful beaks are frequently used to settle territorial disputes. Fishing trips of up to 100 miles are undertaken by either parent and involve diving from a height of some 40 feet into a shoal of fish and can reach a depth of anywhere up to 80 feet. Fish are swallowed whole and partly digested food for chicks is regurgitated straight into open beaks. So well are chicks provided for that they often grow to more than a third larger than their parents. But once fledged that's it; parental care ceases and puppy fat is quickly burnt off finding their own food. It takes a young gannet 4 years to acquire adult plumage and a further 2 years before it breeds. Non-breeding birds nearly always return to their natal colony and occupy an area of their own to one side called the club. This is all stuff you can read about in books but there is nothing to match the experience of being alone amongst these faintly odd but always dignified birds and watching all the little dramas of family life unfold before your eyes.

This adventure occurred 33 years ago and it was only this spring that my acquaintance with Grassholm was renewed, this time from the comfort of a ship. It was late in the day as we passed round the rock. Some birds were returning from their feeding grounds and others filled the sky above the rock, itself made white with nesting birds. The whole scene radiated a very special magic. Earlier that day we had visited Skomer, another island off the coast of Pembrokeshire, where we had spent 2 hours pottering about in a zodiac amongst colonies of puffins, guillemots and razorbills, getting close in under the cliffs where they were nesting. All three species are members of the auk family and were it not for the difference in their bills (guillemots long and pointed, razorbills hawk-like, and puffins famously absurd) it would be difficult to tell them apart. Like gannets all three spend their lives far out at sea, only coming to land to nest. They all dive, duck-like, to catch fish, use their wings to swim under water and by and large they all mate for life. In this regard puffins do best, being helped by the refinement of nesting in the privacy of burrows on the cliff-tops, away from the narrow rock-face ledges where guillemots and razorbills incubate within touching distance and marital commitments are sometimes forgotten under cover of the general free-for-all.

Although auks predominated in the waters around Skomer, there were also gulls, kittiwakes, fulmars and Manx shearwaters. These last are strange, peripatetic sea-birds which, like puffins, nest in burrows, parents incubating in shifts each lasting several days. Seen at close quarters so many breeding birds going about their business creates an atmosphere of frenetic activity. Yet by standing back a little, all this merges into a unified setting of cliffs topped with drifts of wild flowers, rocky coastlines and a clear blue sea so that it would be hard to imagine a spectacle more beautiful or indeed peaceful.

July 2012

What it means to be a bullfinch

Odd things, bullfinches; we seldom see them around the garden and yet every year one pair, never more, turns up out of the blue just as the berries on our amelanchier ripen. Then with a little help from blackbirds, blue tits, the odd pigeon and this year on one precious occasion a male blackcap they strip it bear. It takes about a week and then they are gone as quickly as they came. With their black heads and wings, grey backs, white rumps and red breasts and flanks (a gentle blush pink in the hen) they brighten the place up no end. But why, always, just one pair, why do they come and go together as if joined by string and where are they when not eating our berries? To get some answers we must go to Jurgen Nicholi, an 18-year- old bird enthusiast who, in 1943, enlisted in the German army, was taken prisoner by the British who handed him over to the Belgians and put to work in the coal mines. Released in 1947 Nicholi renewed his love of birds by buying a caged bullfinch and quickly became fascinated by its ability to mimic a human whistle. Thus began a life-long relationship with bullfinches which took Nicholi to Mainz University and eventually to a job working with the famous bird behaviourist Conrad Lorenz. Older readers may remember black and white films on television of Lorenz walking around, followed by geese which he had himself raised and as a result thought he was their mother. Others were of gulls tricked into dropping food onto bits of cardboard cut out and painted to look like the open mouths of their nestlings.

Nicholi knew that in the wild the song of male bullfinches was no more than a feeble cheep. He also knew about the centuries-old tradition of so-called whistling bullfinches which had been trained by foresters in Vogelsberg who took young birds from their nests, hand-reared them and by whistling to them over several months, taught them to mimic songs. Soon the commercial possibilities became apparent and caged birds were taught Dutch and English tunes to widen the market. Nicholi's experiments also demonstrated that these cage-birds, deprived of female companions, became strongly attached to their human alternatives, reacting to the routines of the household in the same way as a pet dog. These endearing habits quickly made whistling bullfinches a "must-have" item amongst ladies of fashion in Victorian London.

But there were three problems; first that teaching these bullfinches to sing was a long and laborious task, further complicated by the inability to pick out singing males from non-singing females at the age at which singing lessons must start. Much time was thus wasted. Second, bullfinches are strangely neurotic birds, sulking and even dropping dead if routines are changed, a trait which was ill-suited to withstanding the rough and tumble of the cage-bird trade. And third, male bullfinches, their macho looks and forthright manner notwithstanding, are poor breeders. Combine this with their feeble song and a courtship routine that amounts to little more than a nudge and a wink and a picture emerges of a bird unbothered by the usual male urge to spread his genes as far and wide as possible. It seems that once he has found a mate, no other male has the will to challenge for ownership, nor does he wish to look elsewhere. Thus the pair are left in peace to spend the rest of their lives together. Energies spent by other birds in sorting out these issues are used by bullfinches to engage in more cerebral matters of which the ability to learn tunes is but one example. Indeed it was the view of Jurgen Nicholi that one day micro-dissection of the bullfinch brain would reveal the physiology by which this is achieved.

Meanwhile we struggle through a summer where each day sees new records in awfulness and this makes things tough for butterflies. Even caterpillars have suffered. They need a body temperature of at least 32° before they can start to feed and in cold weather some achieve this by snuggling up together for mutual warmth. Others find a little sun-trap low down, stretch out on a leaf and hope for the best. Butterflies are slightly better off, requiring a minimum temperature of only 30° to fly. To help achieve this those with dark wings sit with them held flat out on a warm surface. Then by raising and lowering their wings they can control their body temperature. White and blue butterflies, on the other hand, sit with wings held at a **V** above their backs so that sun-rays are deflected onto their bodies. Sunlight is also necessary to enable the compound eyes of butterflies to pick out the colours of those flowers which can provide them with nectar as well as to identify prospective mates. This explains why butterflies only fly when the sun shines. And then there's wind; no butterfly likes being buffeted about by the wind, least of all those which inhabit tree-tops. Such ones are purple emperors which, as I write these notes, should be approaching the high point of their flight season. Last year was a good one for these, the most spectacular of all our native butterflies; that is until the third week in July when the gales came and proceeded to wipe them all out almost over-night.

August 2012

A summer that never was

A few months ago a friend asked me how I would console myself if suddenly all butterflies disappeared. It was more of a tease than a serious question and my reply was like-wise light-hearted. Anyway we were at the time basking in warm March sunshine and there was little to suggest that we were about to enter a prolonged period of foul weather which would put all wildlife under huge pressure. Like moths, butterflies have a four-stage life-cycle in any one of which they are exposed to a range of risks which might, but for their beauty, pass unnoticed. Scientists therefore keep an eye on butterflies, using them much as miners of old used canaries down the pits to warn of the presence of deadly carbon monoxide. So a more thoughtful answer to my friend's question would have been that if butterflies were to disappear completely there would most certainly be underlying reasons of far greater importance than simply their contribution to my enjoyment.

None of this is to suggest that the lack of butterflies this summer conceals the coming of some sort of apocalypse when, in probability, all it does is confirm what we could see for ourselves; that our summer so far has been cold and wet and that this has affected all the normal rhythms of the countryside. For instance, there have been reports of birds starting their autumn migration a month or more early and it is certainly the case that drake mallards in Petworth Park had moulted and gone into their eclipse plumage by mid-July. It may also explain why there are so few dragonflies around, why, also, we had no tadpoles in our pond this year, nor have we seen the customary grass snake there. But butterflies are so much a part of our summer scene that their absence is easily noticed and as the summer has progressed this has been highlighted by an almost complete absence of the magnificos which normally decorate our mid-summer gardens; peacocks, tortoiseshells, commas and brimstones. All these would have been descended from eggs laid by parents coming out of hibernation in the warmth of March and by the time the eggs had hatched into caterpillars temperatures were so low that many would be in a state of torpor and unable to eat. This would have been a serious matter since it is in the caterpillar phase of their life-cycle that butterflies grow, from the size of a pin-head to maybe 2 inches long. This may explain why, amongst those that did make it through to adulthood, there are a fair number which are smaller than usual.

But it's not all bad news; downland butterflies have had a surprisingly good year and in early August on Kithurst Hill chalk-hill blues were up to usual numbers. Woodland butterflies, on the other hand, have suffered more, but by way of consolation all the rain has ensured a wonderful show of flowers. A recent stroll through the woods north of Plaistow which offered the prospect of white admirals, silver-washed fritillaries and the tantalizing possibility of a purple emperor was memorable instead for brilliant splashes betony, knapweed and hemp agrimony. The nearest we came to the elusive purple emperor was via a chance conversation with a couple we bumped into who told us that they had come across a purple emperor a few days before in a woodland glade on Bookham Common, a place just a mile from where we used to live. It was, they told us, the beautiful male with iridescent blue wings shining in the sunlight. It was doing what they often do, imbibing nutritious salts from a pile of fresh horse dung on the path, thus forming an incongruous tableau of extremes in beauty. But it was one which so enchanted our new friends that, having photographed it, they then sat for an hour in the sun watching the butterfly as it moved about in search of the most succulent portions from which to feed, their thoughts in perfect harmony with magic of nature. And if this tale confirms in the minds of any readers a secret belief that those who seek solace in the company of butterflies are at best slightly barmy, I may as well admit that it sparked in me a pang of envy.

So as we come to the end of a summer which has been described by some experts as a catastrophe for butterflies, what of their future? The impact seems to have varied from species to species and the probable causes have not always been the same. So the answer must await the verdict of the experts who will take time to analyse all the data. Some species may take a season or two to recover but we should also remember that our indigenous lepidoptera has survived the vicissitudes of changes in our climate more or less successfully since the ice-age. What they cannot cope with, however, is the assaults on them which come from us humans, either by way of the indiscriminate use of agricultural chemicals or the destruction of their habitat

September 2012

Nature Matters

Life down a hole

Moles, along with their close relatives shrews and hedgehogs, can trace their ancestry back to the dinosaurs. In those days all three probably looked much the same but in the intervening 200 million years some significant changes have taken place; hedgehogs have grown sharp pin-like spikes, the shrewishness of shrews has been enshrined in English literature by William Shakespeare and moles have disappeared beneath the ground, their front paws becoming shovels complete with an extra thumb to facilitate excavation and their blood containing a special protein which enables them to survive in places where oxygen is scarce. Also their fur has come to grow straight up from their skin instead of lying flat in one direction like other mammals. This oddity enables them to run along their tunnels both forward and backward without their hair getting clogged up with earth. It also gives their pelts a soft, velvety feel and because of this farm-workers were once able to make a little extra money catching moles and selling their skins to the fur trade. But after a while the market collapsed; good news for moles, the numbers of which quickly increased, but bad news for gardeners and others who strive to have a decent-looking lawn.

The life-span of a mole is about three years. Each adult has its own network of tunnels little wider than its own body and up to 100 yards long. Some tunnels are so near the surface that the earth is raised up as a ridge; others are up to two feet deep and it is the earth from these that gets shoved up to the surface via vertical shafts and cause the molehills which make such a mess. When moles are excavating they use one front foot to push soil upwards and the other three to provide anchorage. Average burrowing speed is of the order of 15 yards an hour. Although networks are sometimes interconnected, moles are careful not to trespass into a neighbour's territory and if two males accidentally meet there is usually a fight which can sometimes be fatal.

Each mole patrols its private network day and night almost continuously, either increasing its range or searching for food. This consists mainly of earthworms but also includes any tiny invertebrates which happen to fall into its tunnel. Unless a mole eats every few hours it will die of starvation, so in times of plenty worms are caught and stored. The procedure is both gruesome and comical; first their heads are nipped off. This is not fatal but it is sufficient to ensure that the worms lose their sense of direction and cannot escape. It also ensures that the stored food remains fresh and larders of up to a thousand disabled worms have been found. But that is not all; because a worm can regenerate what passes for its brain within about four days and, having done so, could wriggle free, the mole makes things that much more difficult by simply tying the poor thing into a knot. And then finally, before eating it, the mole runs the worm lengthwise through its fingers to force out any earth which may still be lodged in its gut, rather as one might squeeze the remains from a tube of toothpaste.

In the spring when breeding takes place, a male seems able to detect the whereabouts of a prospective mate at some distance even through solid earth. At such times he can burrow short distances at a speed of 50 yards per hour to reach her. But once there he wastes no time because he knows that if he outstays his welcome he risks receiving a nasty bite for his troubles. But this is as nothing compared with the fireworks which are part and parcel of the mating ceremony of shrews, a ritual which often leads to bloodshed and is said to be initiated by the female as a way of testing whether her suitor is sufficiently robust to be worthy of fathering her children. By comparison female moles are at heart sweet-natured animals and will have anticipated the arrival in their burrow of a gentleman by preparing a chamber the size of a football to serve as a birth-chamber and nursery. This they will line with dry grass and leaves collected during one of their infrequent visits to the surface and after a gestation lasting 30 days they will be delivered of a litter of anything up to 7 blind and naked babies. These they will suckle for about 35 days after which they are ready to leave the chamber and venture out into the open in search of a territory of their own.

October 2012

Shrew

Birds in disarray

Once upon a time you could predict the comings and goings of birds with a fair degree of accuracy; summer visitors arrive from the south around April, they build nests, raise families and then leave in August or September, that sort of thing. But recent climatic upheavals have upset these certainties; for example some fieldfares, thrush-like birds which come here from Scandinavia for the winter, this year remained with us to nest rather than return home. Then, by way of contrast, a number of our regular summer visitors found our spring weather so awful that either they delayed nesting or failed altogether and as a consequence autumn departures have varied hugely. And then there is the other group, the winter visitors which breed far to the north and then come back here in the autumn, many of which this year have returned much earlier than usual. A good example is provided by a flock of over 80 black-tailed godwits seen feeding on the tide-line at Pagham Harbour when normally they would still be up in their breeding grounds in Iceland. A pleasant consequence of this was that the males had not yet started their annual moult, thus providing observers with a pleasure seldom accorded to birders in this country of seeing these most elegant of birds still in their chestnut breeding plumage.

But despite all this the grand pattern remains much as usual; huge numbers of birds come here each winter from the north. Distances travelled vary enormously; geese, duck and waders come from as far away as Greenland, Iceland and the White Sea and others come from no further away than colder parts of this country, driven by the search for food. And just to complicate things further, some of our own resident birds are joined for the winter by relatives of the same species from neighbouring countries; thus bitterns from Holland which augment our own sparse population, a few of which usually turn up in January on Burton Mill pond. Other less exciting examples are wood pigeons, blackbirds and various tits and finches from the Baltic and Scandinavia.

Birds are fussy regarding their habitat and around us here we are richly served by the range on offer; woodland, chalk downs, farmland, heaths and wetland; all are here and each draws in its own selection of winter treasures. But right here on our door-step nothing surpasses the wetlands created by the rivers Rother and Arun augmented by the springs and streams which run down off the high weald to the north. Much of this area is now managed by conservation bodies working together to safeguard both the wildlife and, just as important, the beauty of the surrounding landscape. In winter the area holds huge numbers of wigeon and teal along with pintail, gadwell, shoveller, pochard and the ubiquitous mallard. Short-eared owls quarter the reed-beds and meadows near Greatham Bridge. Bewick's swans are often seen grazing on the Amberley Wild Brooks (though mention of them reminds us of the hazards faced by all birds whose migration takes them through hostile territory. Bewick's come from Arctic Siberia and a recent sample of arrivals conducted by the WWT headquarters at Slimbridge showed that 22% of the birds carried gunshot pellets in their flesh. We can only guess at the mortality rate) Large flocks of lapwings take wing whenever a peregrine falcon passes overhead. Snipe and redshank pick around on the fringes of reed-beds and little egrets, recent additions to the British list, survey the scene on long legs. And for twitchers there lurks the ever-present pulse-quickening possibility of a rarity.

For geese, though, a better place is down on the coast amongst the brents from Iceland; seven and a half thousand in Chichester Harbour and two and a half thousand at Pagham alone. Being there on the North Wall at Pagham late in the day when these geese come over low in tight, noisy flocks to roost in safety out on the water is a very special event in the life of any romantic birder. Failing that the best on offer locally are Canada geese and greylags, flocks of which have been much in evidence this autumn. Both species are here all year round and RSPB at Wiggonholt tell me that along the Rother and Arun Valley numbers of Canadas peak at about 7/800 and greylags at 4/500. However, most of these nest elsewhere and numbers around here only start to build up in the autumn. This year they have been much in evidence with daily movements around Fittleworth made up of flocks commuting between autumn stubble where they graze, and water where they bathe and roost. Observation suggests that the reserve at Wiggonholt and its adjacent water meadows on the one hand, and the lakes at Petworth Park, on the other, are focal points with flights between the two either following the course of the Rother or going straight between the two. RSPB tell me that as winter proceeds our local birds disburse in search of new feeding grounds.

And finally a word from the Sussex Ornithological Society to say that they have arranged through the British Ornithological Trust to attach a satellite tag to a cuckoo so that its migration to and from Sussex to Africa can be followed. The plan is that, starting next year, a live map will be displayed with daily up-dates on the SOS web. Similar journeys from other parts of Britain are already up and running and can be followed on www.bto.org/cuckoos. Well worth a look.

November 2012

Nature Matters

Do butterflies have built-in sat-nav?

Many of our smaller butterflies spend their entire lives flying around in circles without ever straying much further than 40 yards from where they were born. But there are at least two species which routinely travel the length and breadth of whole continents and even on occasions cross oceans. One such is the monarch, a butterfly which is widely distributed in North and Central America as well Australasia and parts of Asia. They are strong with a wingspan of 3½ inches and benefit in the battle to survive from an acrid and mildly toxic substance acquired from the milkweed plants which their caterpillars eat. This ensures that all predators give both caterpillar and butterfly a wide berth: all, that is, except the jays and orioles in Mexico which have worked out that the noxious chemicals reside in the black veins in the butterfly's wings. So they simply pull these off and eat the rest.

It is not all that unusual for the odd monarch to turn up here and when one was seen on Portland Bill in late September the press was immediately on to it, pronouncing it a visitor from North America. There are in fact two separate populations in North America, those to the west of the Rockies which spend the winter in Southern California and the rest to the east, the majority, which hibernate in Mexico. These two winter roosts are famous, the butterflies clothing the trees as if they were leaves to create a spectacle which is one of the wonders of the natural world. In the spring both populations spread north in a massive migration all the way up to the Hudson Bay. But because the life-span of each individual is only three weeks the entire journey is accomplished by successive generations working in relays.

Thus it is that the complete round trip can occupy the entire life-span of up to five generations, posing the question as to how these distant descendents find their way back to the same forests which their ancestors left the previous spring. Recent experiments have shown that the butterfly's antennae are used to register the position of the sun and that if this ability is artificially blocked the insect looses its sense of direction. So if it's the sun which guides them, how does the butterfly compensate for the daily movement of the sun across the sky? We do not yet know but one thing is for sure; when cold autumnal air from the Arctic triggers the southward migration, monarch numbers quickly build up into massive swarms as they move down the east coast of America and it is when these swarms encounter strong westerly winds that we here get our visitors. With wind speeds of 30-35 knots the trans-Atlantic crossing takes about four days and it is when these factors coincide that monarchs turn up along our south coast. The record number was in 1999 when 300 were counted and interestingly the same trans-Atlantic winds usually bring us a selection of migrating American birds as well.

The other butterfly in the news recently on account of its peripatetic habits is the painted lady. Those which we see in this country arrive in the spring from the foot-hills of the Atlas mountains. Who can forget the mass invasion here of 2009 when in just two days in May an estimated 28 million crossed the south coast! Like monarchs they lay eggs as they as they travel, leaving their offspring to continue the journey and that year they spread all the way up to Iceland before the season ended. At no stage in the life-cycle of painted ladies can they withstand temperatures lower than -5°. This usually precludes year-round survival north of the Mediterranean, a problem they solve by completing a full life-cycle in just one month without the need to hibernate. Another wintering ground is situated near the Dead Sea from whence painted ladies migrate up through East Europe and on beyond to north Scandinavia. A certain Mr Skerchly who, in 1869, observed the scene whilst out riding his camel, describes it thus;

" presently the pupae began to burst and a myriad of butterflies, limp and helpless, crawled around. And presently the sun shone forth and the insects began to dry and half an hour after birth the whole swarm rose as a dense cloud and flew away eastward towards the sea.... The swarm was certainly more than a mile long and its breadth exceeded a quarter of a mile."

Until recently it was believed that when summer ended and painted ladies had travelled as far north as they could they simply expired. However (and this is what earned them a mention in the papers) new research has revealed that there is a reverse migration which takes place at an altitude of some 1,600 feet and had never before been suspected. This suggests a round trip from North Africa to the Arctic Circle and back of some 9,000 miles and it can be no coincidence that they and the monarchs are considered the world's most successful butterflies: further evidence of the rewards which come to any life-form which has evolved the ability to disperse and increase its distribution.

And finally news from The Grange in Hesworth Lane where a large bat was flying around early in November, long after it should have retired to hibernate. Odder still, it was in the middle of the day and appeared unusually attached to its human observer. Anyone lost a pet bat?

December 2012

In praise of cows & waxwings

Those of us living hereabouts who enjoy a walk in the countryside are spoilt for choice. But if we go where the wildlife is under the management of conservationists we may find that we have grazing cattle for company and this can be a worry if, for instance, we are walking a dog. Nevertheless the hard fact is that grazing farm animals is now a frequently used tool in the management of many different types of habitat and it is no surprise to learn that the Sussex Wildlife Trust themselves own a herd of 70 cattle and more than 600 sheep which they use for just this purpose. Stedham Common, just to the west of Midhurst, is typical of an area of heathland which if left to itself, would gradually be overtaken by mature heather, dank grasses, birch and bracken, and the Trust use their work there as an example to explain exactly how grazing cattle have helped to stem this invasion. Writing in their magazine, they tell us that in the winter the cattle eat mainly gorse, moving to young birch in the spring when the sap is rising. Then in the summer they prefer areas dominated by purple moor-grass which, if left unchecked, would quickly overwhelm more delicate flower species. Add to this the value of trampling hooves which encourages the growth of new shoots of heather as well as churning in wild flower seeds and its easy to see the part they play in the general scheme of things.

The Trust stresses, however, that none of these benefits are, on their own, a complete substitute for mechanical scrub-clearance and suchlike. But they do make a valuable contribution, all the more so if the live-stock is rotated in a way which makes best use of their seasonal grazing preferences. And there is another less obvious role performed by cattle; that of re-distributing nutrients around the grazing area. Simply put, this is achieved by feeding in fertile places where vegetation is lush and then depositing manure where they shelter, usually under trees where nothing much else grows. Ecologists who study these things now focus in detail on micro-habitats and the specialist species associated therewith, so that terms like dung-fauna are freely-used and clearly understood. Good examples of cow-dung-fauna are several species of flies and beetles which in turn attract hornet robber flies. These fearsome-looking insects measure over an inch in length and hang out near cow-pats in order to feed on the other insects that live there. They do this by sucking out their body-fluids having first killed them by injecting a deadly poison. They then lay their eggs in the pile so that their hatching larvae can eat the larvae of other insects which live there. Hornet robber flies now share top billing with field crickets on Lords Piece, attracted, no doubt, by the cattle which graze there from time to time. They fly in July and August and if you happen to encounter one, don't be alarmed by its vicious appearance; it is (according to Wikipedia) harmless to humans.

It has become a habit at this time of year for these notes to remind readers to keep an eye open for waxwings. These unusual-looking birds are the size of plump starlings, are reddish-brown with grey rumps and patches of yellow on their wings and tail and have a prominent crest which sweeps up and back from their forehead. They come over from Scandinavia in the autumn in search of berries and if the crop at home is poor they arrive early and in their thousands and signs are that this could be such a year. The first arrivals were seen in east Scotland in October from whence they have spread progressively south in search of food. By November sightings were coming in from all over the country and as I write, the nearest to us here is Shoreham. Waxwings move around in small flocks and are not too shy to come into towns looking for any berries still on the shrubs. Cotoneasters are a favourite and the birds seem to have learned that these can often be found in public car-parks. where their exotic looks quickly attract attention.

The arrival of visitors here in the south in the second half of the winter is fairly typical of many birds which come into the northern parts of the country early in the winter (or are resident there) and are then driven down to the milder south by hard weather or shortage of food.. Siskins are a good example; we saw them in north Norfolk at the beginning of October but have not yet seen any around here. They come from Scotland, usually arriving in Sussex in the new year and if wild food is plentiful they forage out of sight amongst alders and conifers. For siskins garden nut-feeders are a valuable fall-back. Bramblings are another which had already arrived in north Norfolk by early October and have taken another couple of months to reach us down here. They come here for the winter from Scandinavia in company with their near-relatives, chaffinches, and combined flocks are often seen foraging for mast in beach woods. When disturbed they all fly up into the trees and if bramblings are amongst the flock their white rumps are easy to see.

January 2013

Nature Matters

2012; the ups and downs of a challenging year

The National Trust recently published a review which outlines last year's erratic weather and its effect on our wildlife. What follows is a mixture of bits taken from that review with some local observations and other bits and pieces added.

January- A mild Christmas saw a magnolia in flower on New Year's Day in Cornwell. Short-eared owls which were to be seen quartering the meadows along the Arun valley, prospered all over the country. **February**- An early and mild spring enabled the National Trust to say that on Valentine Day in all their gardens, 19% more flowers were blooming than in 2011. **March**- What turned out to be the best weather of year occurred between 19th and 30th. Large tortoiseshell butterflies, not that rare in central and southern Europe but thought to be extinct in Britain, were seen at Newtown on IOW. Badgers were noticeably short of food. The month ended with the announcement that the two preceding winters had been the driest on record. **April**- On the 4th the jet stream, a high-altitude air-flow which blows eastwards across the north Atlantic and in a normal summer passes well to the north of the British Isles, moved south resulting in the wettest April on record. River bank nesters such as kingfishers and water voles saw their nests flooded and RSPB, Wiggonholt announced that only two nestlings from their resident flock of lapwing survived. Even tree-nesters abandoned sodden nests. The bluebell season came to an early end.

May- Spring fruit blossom was destroyed by wind and rain with knock-on consequences for bees, wasps, hover-flies and, later in the year, berry-eating birds. A brief respite at the end of the month, however, helped some insects. **June-** The incessant rain suited wild flowers with a spectacular display of bee orchids reported from Blakeney in Norfolk and Stackpole Warren in Pembroke: fly orchids did well on Dunstable Downs. In what was generally a bleak time for butterflies the spring hatch of rare wood whites did well in one of their last strongholds in the woods around Chiddingfold. Of our local fritillaries, pearl-bordered and dark green did better than silver-washed which were scarce. The good news was that large blue butterflies, extinct in Britain until just recently, laid record numbers of eggs in a National Trust reserve in Somerset.

July- The monthly rainfall exceeded last year's by 150%. More than 10,000 pyramidal orchids provided spectacular viewing at Sharpenhoe Clappers in the Chilterns. Others to benefit were slugs and snails though they faced competition from giant 4-inch long super-slugs which have recently arrived here on salad plants imported from Spain. These uninvited visitors lay eggs in batches of several hundred which helps them to out-survive our native species. The Olympic Games which straddled July and August continued the mood of national jollification which had started with the Queen's Jubilee and even when the inevitable down-pour arrived the Mayor of London was able to keep the nation's party going by telling us that the rain made the lightly-clad ladies playing beach volley-ball glisten like wet otters. But I stray from my brief as your Nature Correspondent; more apposite is the extent to which science, when applied to training, can help the human body endlessly to improve its athleticism. Nowhere was this better exemplified than when Mo Farah won the 5000 meter race watched by Rodger Bannister, the man who, in 1954 became the first to run a mile in less than 4 minutes. Bannister had achieved this feat with the help of two close friends in a carefully choreographed run the sole purpose of which was to get him over the line in under 4 minutes. Farah, on the other hand, had to deal with all the tactical manoeuvrings of world-class competitors each intent on winning. Yet a little-reported fact was that he too had covered the last mile (that is, just one section of his 5000 meter race) in under 4 minutes. **August**- Swifts, which gather food for their young by sweeping up beaks-full of insects as they fly, were unable to find sufficient to sustain their broods so that nestlings were left to starve and parents returned early to Africa. Bees and wasps were predictably hit by the poor spring but downland flowers were lush, providing ideal conditions for a heavy hatch of chalk-hill blue butterflies.

September- Warm and sunny weather brought a welcome number of red admiral and large white butterflies though it is hard to tell whether these were ones which should have hatched earlier but were delayed by adverse mid-summer weather or late migrants from across the Channel.. **October**-.Wild food was scarce so that mice, birds and others were scrounging food from pheasant feeder bins. Under-fed mammals such as hedgehogs and bats were going into hibernation dangerously short of body-weight. (Perhaps this explains why a bat was still flying in a Fittleworth garden in November.) Excellent autumn colours brought a pleasant glow to the countryside. **November-** At Blakeney seal pups break the 1000 barrier and include rare twins. A cold snap froze over some local lakes and two male goosanders arrived on the lower lake in Petworth Park, creating a scene reminiscent of a Scottish loch. **December-** more floods. Sightings of waxwings were increasingly common across the south of England but seemed to be giving Fittleworth a miss; that is until the wet and windy morning of 28th when Quentin Gilpin phoned to say that, at that very moment, at least two were feeding on berries in his Greatpin Croft garden and I got there in time to be able to spend some time in the company of these exotic visitors from Scandinavia. Thus ended a most extraordinary and challenging year for wildlife. And so to… **January- 2013-** A sunny day on the 3rd brought out 2 red admiral butterflies which fed peacefully on our mahonia.   February 2013

Nature Matters

Birds doing their best in difficult times

The weather was so warm on 3rd January that butterflies were flying. Then began an extended period of snow and freezing winds which is still going on right up to the closing date for this edition of the magazine. For birds such extremes are confusing and makes the finding of food difficult, Berries were anyway scarce this year and have now all been eaten and if open ground becomes frozen foraging for insects is difficult. Typical victims have been fieldfares and redwings which have been roaming the countryside in large flocks searching for anything they can find. Some have been so desperate that they have even come onto garden bird feeders. Others in the same plight have been pied wagtails which, in competition around the feeders with the likes of sparrows, chaffinches and robins, have revealed a surprisingly aggressive side to their nature. Stock doves have also dropped in from time to time to pick around under the bird table. Smaller and a darker grey than wood pigeons and lacking their white neck markings, stock doves nest in crevasses or bowls in trees and sometimes, too, abandoned rabbit holes. In fact there was a time when people in East Anglia turned this last habit to their advantage by placing sticks across the entrance to the holes to form a grid. This way they imprisoned the young without preventing their parents from feeding them; a strategy that ensured that the squabs were fattened up nicely for the pot.

The intensely cold nights have caused a flock of about a dozen long-tailed tits to establish a night-time snuggery under a conifer near the house. It is well-known that these tiny birds often cuddle up together in an old nest to keep warm at night but it was a surprise to see in a recent edition of Winter-Watch on television several of them fluffing up together to form a ball which seemed to work just as well. Waxwings have continued to excite both birders and casual observers alike. On January 22nd a flock of 20 spent the afternoon in Bury and a large gathering of them on the coast in Kent caused speculation that they might be about to depart for France. If they do, let us hope that the French can curb their appetite for turning anything which is pretty and has feathers into paté.

Other examples of birds dislocated by the weather have been a gannet which should have been fishing miles out at sea but instead was on a flooded gravel pit near Aldershot and another which flew over Mitcham Common. Then came news that a snow goose from North America had joined the wintering pink-footed geese on the mud-flats at Morecombe Bay. These geese turn up here unexpectedly from time to time and always cause a stir. But what makes this one extra special is that instead of being pure white it is a rare variant in which all but the head is blue. Then there is the case of the hoopoe, a bird which spends the winter in Sub-Saharan Africa, coming to Europe in April and very occasionally straying across the Channel. So imagine the surprise when one turned up during the first week of February in a garden in Poole.

The least sign of spring is sufficient to make the juices rise as we saw one day in January when walking round Frensham pond in Surrey. The weather, as usual, had been dreadful but a rare patch of sunshine was enough to get a pair of great crested grebes out on the water to perform their uniquely spectacular courtship routine It went like this; first the male dived down and collected a beak-full of water-weed. This he presented to his prospective mate in a ceremony which involved the pair facing one another, breasts touching, bodies and necks at full stretch and crests erect. Various affectionate waggling of the heads was followed by the pair paddling off over the surface of the water, side by side, bodies and necks still held high in a display of both mutual and self-admiration.

But this was premature and it seems we must wait a little longer for the true harbinger of spring, the shamelessly parasitic cuckoo. Each female lays a total of about 12 eggs one at a time in the nests of various host-birds. With each laying the cuckoo removes one egg from the host nest so that the clutch remains the same size. This is achieved either by swallowing the egg or taking it away in its beak to be smashed later. When hatched the cuckoo chick quickly outgrows the host chicks and as it does so it heaves them out of the nest until it is the only one left. But here's the odd thing; it is well-known that all nestlings learn the calls and songs as well as the ability to identify their own species by associating with their siblings and parents. These vital lessons are learned during the first few days of life. So how is it that cuckoos don't sing like their foster-parents and, when mature, try to mate with that same species?

Alan Root, the famous wildlife photographer, tells a story which may help with the answer. It concerns a crowned crane which had been brought to him as an orphaned chick to join a young hippo, an anteater and other waifs and strays which already lived with him and his wife in their garden in Kenya. These extended family members lived happily together and in due course the crane grew into a graceful metre-tall pale grey male with a fine golden-crested head. But there was a problem; although Lake Naivasha was nearby he could not find a mate. So instead he fell in love with the leaden grey standpipe with a shiny brass tap which stood in the middle of the lawn and was his height. Every day the crane danced, pirouetted and waved its wings in front of the unresponsive tap. He even brought gifts of grasshoppers shoving them into the tap opening, all to no avail. There is, though, a happy ending; eventually a real, live female crested crane joined the party and the two raised a family down on the lake. But the episode does question the efficiency of parental imprinting.

March 2013

Owls; facts and fantasies

When Edward Lear used an owl to add whimsy to his poem about the owl and the pussycat which went to sea in a beautiful pea-green boat. he was doing no more than following in the footsteps of story-tellers and fantasists down the centuries. In fact in the mythology of ancient Greece Athene, the Goddess of Wisdom, was said to have been so impressed by the solemn and wise appearance of the little owls which inhabited the Acropolis that she banished the crows to make more room and announced that the owls were her favourite birds. Word soon spread that the all-seeing eye that bestowed upon the Goddess her divine insights was the same as that which enabled owls to see by night, and thus it was that little owls were accorded a special status in contemporary Greece. Coins bore their image and if one were to fly over the field of battle a Greek victory was assured. To this day these associations are enshrined in the scientific name for a little owl which is *Athene noctura*, meaning literally "Athene by night"

World-wide there are about 200 different species of owl with distribution everywhere except Antarctica and a few places in Greenland. They range in size from eagle owls which are larger even than buzzards down to starling-sized pygmy owls Most fly at night but some also at dusk and during the day. They are, however, different to non-owl raptors such as falcons and hawks and it is precisely these differences which and have earned owls a special place in literature and folklore. Their upright posture and large intense binocular eyes give them a bearing which demands our attention but also restricts their field of view. So owls have evolved a unique structure in their necks that enables them to rotate their heads by a full 270° without moving their bodies.and this has led to stories that if an owl fixes you in its relentless gaze and you find the experience unnerving, just walk in a circle around it and it will strangle itself.

Sound is even more important to hunting owls than sight so they have developed flat faces that are fringed by feathers to form a saucer, an arrangement which reflects sound back into their ears. Several owl species also have tufts of feathers on top of their heads which look like ears and this has lead to two species being called respectively long eared owls and short eared owls. But these feathers are no more than adornments, albeit ones which add to the impression of worldly wisdom which characterises all owls. Add to this their soft feathers which render all flight completely silent and calls that include hoots, grunts, shrieks and hisses and it is easy to see how it is that these birds of the night so often feature in folklore, their roles ranging from the comical, wise and cuddly to the eerily frightening and spooky according to the needs of the story.

But there is another thing about owls that is definitely fact and this concerns the way they handle their food; whereas other raptors tear the meat off their prey using a powerful beak, owls swallow theirs whole and regurgitate the indigestible bits later in the form of pellets. These pellets can be collected and, if soaked in water, the bones can be separated from the fur and feathers to reveal what the bird has been eating. The beautiful thing about all this is that the tiny bones are almost always intact. Even the jaw-bones usually retain a full set of teeth. It is therefore possible to bleach these remains in brine and then mount them on card using a spot of glue. They can then be arranged in such a way as to replicate a skeleton complete with limbs, spine, ribs and skull. Working on the supposition that each pellet is derived from one kill the fun is then to identify the prey-animal which may have been a mouse or vole or shrew. As a small boy living on a farm which had several owl territories within it, I spent many happy hours studying these things - a pursuit which had the added attraction that it provoked my mother into saying that the whole escapade was not only a pointless waste of time but also mildly revolting.

However just in case this idea catches on, squeamish workers might wish guidance to help ensure that what they have found in the course of their country walks is indeed an owl pellet. The following notes are, therefore offered to avoid unpleasant surprises. Owl pellets are dry and consist mainly of knotted fur amongst which and clearly visible, are bones and beetle wings. Except in the case of little owls, pellets are regurgitated around favourite roosts and are therefore found in concentrated areas. The pellets of barn owls are found around their nests, measure 30-65 mm x 18-24 mm. and have a varnished appearance. Those of tawny owls are the same size but are grey and friable and are always deposited some distance from the nest. Those of little owls are the same colour as those of the tawny owl but are smaller and sometimes taper to a thread. And as a final guide, if your dog roles in it, it is not what you are looking for.

And finally a word of thanks to Beth for including in last month's "Around The Garden" a list of plants which attract butterflies and, just as important, for her plea to gardeners to leave space for a few nettles. All this reminds me to report that one Sunday this February our Rector's wife Sally was disturbed during morning service by a tortoiseshell butterfly which had fluttered into her pew and then promptly gone back into its winter-long sleep. These butterflies, along with peacocks and red admirals, are the ones which wake up from hibernation when the weather warms up and then look for the tender young nettles on which to lay their eggs. These eggs hatch into the caterpillars which eat the nettles and become the mid-summer butterflies which feed on the nectar provided by the plants so kindly listed by Beth. And so it goes on.

April 2013

Life in a pond

Anything from a huge lake to the smallest garden pond holds an astonishing array of wildlife. Even the surface of a butt full of stagnant rain water, unless kept covered, quickly becomes a seething mass of mosquito larvae, to say nothing of the odd water-snail and beetle. Many of the things which live in water are too small to see with the naked eye but even the smallest organism plays a role which is vital to the maintenance of a habitat in which all can survive. There are, broadly speaking, two types of fauna which inhabit ponds; those, like fish, which live out their entire lives, both as egg and adult, in water, and those with more complicated lifecycles which switch from water to land as they pass through the stages. The most obvious examples of the latter are frogs, toads and newts which, as adults are terrestrial but come to water in the spring to mate and lay their eggs, sometimes in a large procession which follows the same route each year. Indeed some readers may remember about 20 years ago when a culvert which runs from the lower pond in Petworth Park under the A283 and out the other side, was due for a spring-clean. Word of this reached the Petworth Society who knew that this culvert was used by toads to cross under the road and into the pond. So, anxious for their welfare, the Society organised a rota of members to carry them across by the bucket-full, not telling their members until after they had volunteered that these movements only occur at night.

The eggs of frogs are contained within a foamy jelly called spawn, those of toads form strings attached to pond vegetation and those of newts are laid singly, usually wrapped in an under-water leaf. In warm weather eggs hatch in a few days and the tadpoles of all three, when young, look much the same. As babies they feed on algae but as they grow they eat fish eggs and even each other. After about four months the tadpoles of frogs and toads loose their tails, grow legs and climb from the pond to start life on land. By then their gills have disappeared and they extract oxygen from the air using newly-formed lungs. Newt tadpoles, on the other hand, use their tails for swimming and so retain them for the rest of their lives. But unlike frogs and toads, young newts remain in the water until mature which may take up three years. During this time they spend the winter in semi-hibernation buried deep within the debris at the bottom of the pond. Here they may be joined by the odd male frog who believes that by returning to the pond in the autumn rather than waiting until the spring rush he will be in pole position when the ladies return. This choice obliges him to shut down all but the most essential body processes and maintain the simplest of lives by absorbing oxygen from the water through his skin – a risky business at the best of times but fatal if the water is shallow and freezes over so that toxic gasses build up.   .

Many insects use water for part only of their life-cycles. Dragonflies and damselflies are good examples, adults laying eggs throughout the summer, attaching them to the stems of aquatic plants just below the water-line. These hatch into nymphs and as such they can remain in water for up to three years sleeping through the winter deep in the mud. They are voracious eaters, their menu consisting of anything small enough for their powerful jaws to handle. This includes the nymphs of any other dragonfly smaller than themselves. When fully developed the nymph climbs up the stem of any handy plant into the fresh air and breaks free from the hard outer case in which it has lived. At first the adult which now emerges looks not unlike the nymph which preceded it, but soon wings appear, the body grows and the insect takes on a beautiful iridescent glow.

There is a certain magnificence about dragonflies which is perhaps enhanced by the knowledge that they are little changed since, 300 million years ago, they were amongst the first insects to fly on earth. They hunt with three pairs of legs held forward to form a kind of basket with which they scoop up the air-borne insects which form their food. Their eyes, so large that they meet together over their foreheads, are made up of hundreds of tiny lenses which gives them a mosaic appearance and provides a 360° view. Their two pairs of wings can be moved independently and this enables the insect to hover or to fly either backwards or forwards, sideways or up and down. This wonder of biological engineering is the final stage the life-cycle and will last at best until winter sets in. So if the next generation is to be secured finding a mate and laying eggs is an urgent matter, and this is a time when you often see couples flying around with the male still holding the female with whom he has just mated firmly by the scruff of her neck and dunking her, tail-first, in the water. This odd behaviour is no more than the male supervising the laying of her eggs, a strategy which enables him to be sure that these are the eggs which bear his and only his genes.

Other insects such as water beetles, water bugs, water boatmen and pond skaters, although able to travel overland from one pond to another, live their lives either immersed in water or on its surface. Add to this the many animals which visit to find food such as, say, grass snakes. They are good swimmers but cannot breathe underwater. Their jaws are hinged in a way which allows a huge gape sufficient to swallow frogs and fish with ease. Other visitors are herons and in the more secluded ponds mallard and moorhens. This wide range of species will quickly find its way to any suitable stretch of water and inevitably the normal rules which govern a community of wildlife prevail; that is to say there is a constant battle for survival. Things eat each other and this makes the management of ponds intended purely for ornamental fish and precious aquatic plants something of a problem. May 2013

Nature Matters

Spring birds & racing snails

Just as we thought the worst was over, along comes the coldest March for fifty years, and so it has remained for most of April and now into May. So perhaps it was no surprise that some of the winter-visiting birds stayed with us longer than usual before heading back up north. A good example was a flock of waxwings seen in Hove on 22nd April. Siskins, too, were still on bird feeders here in Fittleworth long after they should have departed. Cold weather, however, seems to have had less effect on the arrival of summer visitors and the pair of swallows which return each spring to reclaim their nest in Janet and Patrick Hester's garage in Little Bognor arrived on 14th April, the earliest ever recorded and by early May all the usual summer visitors were here, including such habitual laggards as swifts and spotted flycatchers. Some people say there are more blackcaps than usual and this may be because some come here just for the winter, some just for the summer and a few stay all year round. So if spring arrivals got here before spring leavers had left numbers would, for a while, have been higher than usual.

A feature of this spring has been an unusual number of rarities seen, especially during the third week in April, although whether this indicates a shift in distribution or simply an increase in the number of knowledgeable birders constantly on the look-out is uncertain. First up was a Bonelli's warbler at Pagham. If I had seen this bird I would have called it a willow warbler but any birder who had holidayed in or around the Adriatic would have noted its paler flank and slightly smaller size and known better. Word of this got out on the internet and birders from all over quickly gathered to see this rare visitor and inevitably with so many experts gathered in one place other rarities were spotted. Two such were a long-eared owl skulking deep on a nearby bush and a common rosefinch from north-east Scandinavia or perhaps Russia, the latter particularly prized by twitchers. But no great expertise would have been needed to identify the purple ibis which was also on the near-by water-meadows at Warningcamp. This is a bird the beauty of which would catch the eye of even the most casual observer. Much like a small heron but with a long down-curved beak and dark plumage which in summer gleams with a purple sheen, it is a bird of the coastal marshes in south and south-eastern Europe and Africa. Its presence on the outskirts of Arundel, therefore, caused understandable excitement.

Add to these unusual visitors the pied flycatcher which was seen on the golf course at Selsey, another summer visitor probably on its way to the species UK stronghold in the Forest of Dean. Then came the red-rumped swallow, more at home in the high mountains of Spain but this April hunting for insects over Waltham Meadows. Meanwhile here in Fittleworth redpolls were busy at a nyger feeder in Wyncombe Close and a red-legged partridge was foraging amongst the straw bales in the field just below Sandy Lane. And then there was the hobby, a graceful little falcon which accompanies swallows coming up each spring from

Africa, catching and eating them on the wing, which dropped in to give our bird-table the once over. And finally red kites which now seem to be a regular part of the local bird scene with sightings spreading right along the downs. These spectacular birds are the size of a buzzard but with their more slender, pointed wings, forked tail and languid flight are quite distinctive. Though they sometimes kill small mammals and small birds and can often be found foraging for earthworms their staple food comes from scavenging and at a time when raptors in general are blamed for the declining populations of prey-species it is worth remembering that in 18th century England their role in clearing up putrefying rubbish earned them protected status. As an example, the recent birth of a calf in a field near the Roman Villa at Bignor quickly attracted the attention of four red kites which came in to make the most of the after-birth but paid no attention to the new-born calf just a few yards away.

So now the scene shifts to a village pub in Derbyshire which each New Year's day, we hear, is the venue for a maggot race. The course is a board the size of a tea-tray, divided length-wise into channels which prevent the contestants from straying. The race is started by shining a light from behind and the whole thing hinges upon the tendency of a maggot to move away from an area of bright light towards the safety of shade. Our reporter, the former MP, writer and broadcaster Matthew Parris, tells us in *The Times* that the event brings in people from far and wide and that passions arouse accusations of nobbling which fly back and forth between sponsors. His suggestion that maggots might be decorated with the racing colours of their sponsors was well-received but not so his idea that racing form should be analysed and used to breed future winners. The difficulty of tracking the lineage through successive generations from maggot to fly to egg and back to maggot prompted the comment that perhaps he was taking things too seriously. But even so the general idea, surely, suggests possibilities for fund-raising here in Fittleworth, an idea which might be mulled over by, say, the Friends of St Mary's. A maggot race with entrants sponsored by local well-wishers, perhaps, as a side-attraction at our next Harvest Supper would certainly be a novelty. Or we could replace the maggots with snails to provide a gardening theme. The event could then be staged, for example, in tandem with a guest speaker at the Horticultural Society AGM. That way Beth could offer a gardener's knowledge about the ways of snails and with expertise, also available within the village, from both the Hong Kong Jockey Club and the world of Formula One motor racing to add some essential razzmatazz, the possibilities seem endless.

June 2013

Nature Matters

Two squabbles and then briefly summer

It was a sunny afternoon and we were having tea in the garden. Earlier that day at Lords England had bundled New Zealand out for 86 to win the first Test match of the summer. The three ladies were quietly talking and contentment was in the air. I, for my part, was watching a magpie foraging in the newly sown field just over the fence. Then something occurred even more astonishing than the cricket; the bird suddenly flew up in pursuit of what looked at first like a piece of brown paper caught in the wind. But it wasn't that at all: it was a bat. For the next minute or so the bird chased the bat, the two twisting and turning until eventually the bat was able to make a rather undignified escape, whereupon the magpie returned to its foraging as if nothing had happened. So what on earth was going on? Small mice and the like are part of a magpie's diet and it seems reasonable, therefore, that a grounded bat could be taken for a meal. Also bats, although essentially nocturnal, often resort to day-time hunting, especially in cold weather when few insects are out at night, or when females are building themselves up in readiness for giving birth in July.

But none of this quite explains what it was that triggered an aerial combat which I had just seen. Nevertheless the event reminds me of one of the first stories ever related on this page back in October 1996. I recounted, then, an incident that occurred when Bridget and I were walking along the river. It was a bright sunny afternoon and we were, once again, surprised to find a bat flying in daylight backwards and forwards, over the surface of the water, obviously catching insects. Bridget had her camera with her and, encouraged by the regular pattern of flight, immediately fancied her chances of getting the sort of photograph which, if successful, would have been a sure prize-winner. The bat, however, had other ideas; it immediately abandoned its hunting routine and instead flew straight towards Bridget. She, by this time, was so busy searching for the bat through the view-finder of her camera that she never saw it coming. So imagine her startled surprise when I told her that if she moved slowly and gave me the camera I was now better able to photograph the bat than she because it had just landed on her tummy and, head-down, had gone straight to sleep. True, I promise!

Anyway, about a week after the magpie/bat affair there was another set-to which greeted me when I drew back our bedroom curtains. At first all I could see was a crow pecking fiercely at something hidden in the long grass in the field.. But it soon became obvious that whatever was down there was fighting back just as fiercely. Then after a while the crow's opponent came into view, and blow me down if it wasn't a tawny owl! The poor thing had clearly come off second best and was trailing a wing as it hobbled off into the sanctuary of a near-by hedge. Soon, however, it was sufficiently recovered to fly up and spend the rest of the morning asleep in our oak tree. In the meantime the crow had been watching events from a near-by fence post. But as soon as the owl flew away it went straight back to the scene of battle and started once again to peck and tug violently at something on the ground. At that stage I had to abandon my observation and it was only several hours later when I went out to see what had been going on that I found the remains of a nearly full grown rabbit in the grass.

So clearly the squabble had been over the possession of a kill. But then the question arises, who or what killed the rabbit in the first place? Unlikely to have been the tawny owl because they confine themselves to small birds and small rodents which they have killed themselves. And certainly not the crow which feeds almost exclusively on carrion with the occasional small rodent thrown in. And another thing; by the time I got to the scene all that remained of the rabbit was the four leg-bones stripped bare of flesh, part of the backbone and a little bit of gut. No skull, no ribs and no skin. So where had all that gone?

Not long ago we were told that spring 2013 had been the coldest for 61 years. But, as always, there were winners as well as losers. Foremost amongst the winners were wild flowers. Cowslips and primroses excelled but the best of all were the bluebells. A good place for these were the woods around Horncroft where they wanted to build the sand quarry a couple of years ago. A high point for us was a walk through there the week after our Village Garden Trail. Sunlight passing through trees about to break into leaf gave everything a soft greenish tint. Patches of primroses and stitchwort peeped through the bluebells and the pale yellow of two female brimstones completed the scene. We watched these butterflies fluttering around a buckthorn tree, gently feeling each leaf bud with outstretched feet to see if it was a suitable place for a caterpillar to grow up. If so, the butterfly settled for a brief second, bent its abdomen down and deposited one tiny egg on the twig just below the bud before flying off to find the next place. Caterpillars will hatch within two weeks by which time the buds will have opened into tender new leaves, just right for them to eat. And as they grow these caterpillars in turn become food for warblers with hungry nestlings to feed. Those that survive turn into the beautiful yellow butterflies which come to take nectar from our late summer flowers and when autumn turns to winter they bury themselves, perfectly camouflaged, deep in ivy where they remain until the next spring.

July 2013

There's more to it than a name

A few weeks ago the television series Springwatch had pictures of a man looking into a net which he had just dragged along the bottom of a pond. As we expected it came up full of small aquatic animals mixed up with weed. In fact the only surprise was that he told us not to worry too much about what everything was called but instead just marvel that such a wide array of life could be jammed into so small a space. It made me wonder if his deeper thought might have been that everything in the net, indeed he himself, we his audience and for that matter the dog sitting on my knee and the bunch of flowers on the table in front of me, are all descended from the same ancestors dating back some 3,600 million years to when we were all single-cell organisms. Maybe he was suggesting that we should marvel at the ancestral journeys that we have all made to get where we are today.

So pursuing this line let us first re-scale those 3,600 million years down to one calendar year. Seen thus, it was not until mid-November that primitive life came out of the water and onto dry land where competition forced adaptation and the creation of many different species. Dinosaurs dominated until early on Christmas morning when a cooling of the earth wiped them out and mammals moved to the forefront. Soon thereafter (on our time-scale) certain forest-dwelling primates came out onto the plains and, the better to see their enemies, stood upright and walked on their hind-legs. By early evening on New Year's Eve ancestral man was beginning to cultivate crops and by mid-night he had created the world as we know it today. Whilst many lower animals have innate abilities far in advance of humans, the unique inventive ingenuity of the latter has enabled them to develop the tools which maintain his status as leading species.

The task of adapting to changing conditions faced by all wildlife never ends and is driven by random mutations (abnormal characteristics which are inheritable) which are tested in the battle for survival. Those that confer an advantage in the struggle for survival are passed on to future generations and slowly spread through the species. Thus it is that giraffes have gradually developed longer and longer necks which provides the advantage of being able to browse amongst tree-tops, cockroaches can digest cellulose, giving them a wider choice of places to live, and the water fleas in that man's net could be any one of the 600 or so which are sufficiently different from each other to be called a species in their own right.

Nature provides many examples of how plants and animals have improved their chances of survival. Horns, antlers, claws, tusks and fangs have all been developed for hunting, self-defence and herd dominance. Defence of territory often leads to fierce battles and seems to be a trait that has been retained by mankind as Matt Rudd notes in his book *A Field Guide To The English* where he tells us that at any given time in this country some 17,000 neighbours are at loggerheads over the positioning of boundary hedges. Another survival adaptation has been that of mimicry. This is well exemplified by hoverflies, a stingless group of flies which seek safety by mimicking wasps and bees. Monarch butterflies provide another example; because their caterpillars eat the leaves of milkweed they taste nasty and birds avoid them. So other butterflies that have, as an accident of birth, inherited wings that look like those of a monarch have also prospered. And just to show how widespread mimicry is we should not forget the early European colonists with postings to the east who, in their anxiety to command respect and unquestioning obedience from their charges, grew facial hair groomed to mimic the fierce visage of the local alpha-male monkeys.

Nature also throws up examples where the physical adaptation goes hand-in-glove with behaviour. For instance rattle snakes have developed a loose bone held within a dry sack of skin located in its tail. When shaping up for a kill the snake raises its tail and shakes it. This makes a rattling sound which attracts the attention of its prey. The snake then manoeuvres its head unseen into position and does the business. Conjurers and pickpockets operate in much the same way. But the prize for versatility and general cunning goes to the large blue butterfly. The story starts with a young caterpillar eating thyme. But its long-term strategy is to trick its way into the nest of red ants of the species *Myrmica sabulati.* So when it is no more than a few hours old it drops to the ground, always late in the day when these ants forage for food. (Other ants forage mostly in the morning). When the right ant finds the caterpillar it knows that by massaging a gland on its back it can extract a nutritious secretion which it laps up. What the ant does not know, however, is that the secretion also contains a chemical which mimics the pheromone used by ants to recognise each other. So when the caterpillar also changes shape to resemble an ant grub the ant is tricked into thinking it has found a stray from its nest. So it picks up the fraudulent caterpillar and carries it back to the nest. Once integrated into the ant community the caterpillar then starts to eat the genuine grubs which it still mimics, taking care not to provoke the animosity of the worker ants. This can go on for two years by which time it has becomes 100 times its original size. When it eventually pupates it begins once again to exude the nutrients which the ants find so attractive and maybe this is what seals the bond between the two because when the butterfly hatches a procession of ants accompany it from the nest and stand guard whilst it dries its wings and makes ready to fly. Nevertheless not all ant colonies tolerate this extraordinary behaviour and survival rates are low. For this reason large blues became extinct here in 1979. However in a triumph of conservation based on the knowledge that the survival rate is 5 times greater in the nests of the red ant *Myrmica sabuleti* than in any other, a programme of re-introductions has resulted in the establishment of several new colonies scattered along the chalk downs of southern England..

August 2013.

Grasshoppers & crickets

It would probably be pushing things a bit to place the chirrups of crickets and grasshoppers alongside the song of a lark as the quintessence of an English summer but most people would agree that without these sounds the summer countryside would seem empty. And it adds something to know that these two closely-related insects with an ancestry going back 200 million years, turn up everywhere outside the polar regions and are represented by more than 20,000 different species. Classed collectively as orthoptera, they can be divided broadly into two distinct ecological types; those which are adapted for life in the open and those which live a life largely of concealment, often below ground.

The former are in constant danger of attack from a wide range of predators and have therefore developed various strategies for survival. Some rely on camouflage and others have made themselves distasteful to predators by eating foods which make them distasteful to predators. Most have keen hearing and good eyesight which provide early warning of approaching danger. Long, powerful legs facilitate a rapid escape and some have brightly coloured wings which are revealed only in flight. Flashing these frightens would-be attackers and, as a refinement, some species, when flying, have learnt to fold them out of sight and then glide on a few extra yards before landing. This way they fool pursuers into searching for them in the wrong place. I was a victim of this ruse once long ago when trying to photograph a grasshopper with attractive red wings on a blisteringly hot day in France. When eventually I did find one settled on the bare ground its camouflage was so good that it was almost impossible to pick out and certainly not worth a photograph.

Orthopterans that live largely subterranean lives fall into three distinct groups. The first are those which either burrow into soil or live in rotting wood or beneath stones. Their limited sorties into the open are usually at night. Their legs are short and shovel-like and their bodies cylindrical and smooth. Then come the cave-dwellers, delicate insects, dull-coloured and with extremely long legs. Their eyesight is poor but their other senses are excellent. And finally there are the few orthopterans which spend their entire lives underground. Some of these are soft, unpigmented and blind and have legs entirely adapted for digging. Amongst these are mole crickets (of which more in a minute) and ant crickets. Ant crickets are very small, flattened, wingless insects which live their lives in the nests of ants, feeding from secretions produced by their hosts.

Most, but not all orthopterans produce a sound which, technically, is called stridulation but, simply put, is a song. It is usually only males which stradulate and it is their way of whistling up females. Thus it is important that only females of the same species respond and so each species has its own song, received by their ladies whose ears, incidentally, are placed in their legs. A further safeguard against miscegenation is the unique courtship dances practised by males. These, too, are attractive only to females of the same species. Songs are produced in two different ways. In one specialized veins in the base of the wings are rubbed together to produce a tooth and comb effect and the other involves friction between a ridge of pegs on the inside of the hind leg and veins on the forewing.

Neither of these processes should be confused with that which is used by cicadas, something familiar to anyone who has spent a night within earshot of a Mediterranean olive grove. Cicadas produce their song by using muscles located within their abdomens to stress and flex two membranes, the sound thus made then being amplified by air-sacks. This process is much the same as that developed by the Australian entertainer Ralph Harris using a thing he called a wobbleboard to accompany his songs from the Aussie outback. Which brings us back to mole crickets, represented in this country by just one fairly rare species. Word is that a male has been stridulating this summer in a garden in Little Bognor and those hearing it probably already know that mole crickets build the entrance to their burrows in a shape which matches in astonishing detail the most up-to-date loudspeakers computer-designed by man. Thus enhanced, their stradulations are often audible from over a mile away.

Grasshoppers which inhabit the arid wastes surrounding the North African and American desert deserve special mention. Solitary and miserable, they scratch out a meagre living as best they can. Then the rains come and the females start to lay eggs; the larvae which hatch have an abundance of food and become adults much larger and more robust than their parents. They soon eat everything and become restless, so gather into swarms and look for new places to feed. Swarms congregate and soon number 50 thousand million insects, now better known as locusts. Those in the centre of the swarm move to the outside but venture no further, so the swarm stays as a cohesive but directionless whole at the mercy of the wind. If blown over farmland the destruction wrought is legendary. But if they meet barren land or the sea they perish, leaving just a few survivors to revert to the miserable existence of those that started the whole process in the first place.

And to finish, here is a heart-warming story about a pair of swallows that built a nest in the roof timbers of the garage at Mill House. All went well until the eggs hatched whereupon the strain of a growing family proved too much for the nest and it fell, broken, to the floor. Luckily help was on hand; the nest was re-constructed in a shoe-box and, with young inside, placed on a handy nearby surface. The parents immediately resumed their duties, the young survived and by the time you read this will be safely on their way to Southern Africa.

September 2013.

Butterflies bounce back

Early in July it would have required a brave person to predict that we were on the verge of a good old fashioned summer and with it an explosion of butterflies. After all we had just come through several months of appalling weather when butterflies had been alarmingly thin on the ground and birders had started to talk about a songless spring. On top of this, the U.K. Butterfly Monitoring Scheme had just published a report that laid out fair and square the damage that the cold wet summer of 2012 had inflicted upon our butterflies. It told us for instance that 52 of the 56 species found in this country had declined year on year, in many cases by more than 50%, and that, in a controlled sample, 300,000 fewer butterflies had been counted than in 2011. Common species had suffered just as much as the rare ones and for those already struggling there was the very real fear that last year's hit would prove fatal.

So when this year also got off to a poor start expectations were low and even when, early in July, there was a hint that things were improving, people remained sceptical. Then a letter in the papers from a man in the midlands said that in the course of a woodland walk he had counted a record thirty purple emperors, a number which, occurring as it did at the extreme northern limit of their range, would have been surprising in any year. So when news came through of strong hatches in the woods around Chiddingfold and Dunsfold which are purple emperor strongholds and this was followed by a deluge of many other mid-summer butterflies, it really did seem that something big was under way. Soon such favourites as small tortoiseshells, peacocks, commas and brimstones were appearing as if from nowhere. Even in our little patch of wild flowers common blues, small coppers and brown argus were flying after an absence of three years and have laid eggs and a white admiral which wandered into the garden at Wyncombe Hill got its photograph taken. Migrants from across the Channel such as red admirals, clouded yellows and painted ladies have been plentiful and have even included such rarities as long-tailed blues and swallowtails, the latter not *britannicus*, the sub-species which breeds in Norfolk and flies in May but *gorganus* from the Continent. The nearest was seen in a garden in Steyning.

To appreciate the full glory of all these mid-summer butterflies we should put to one side any prejudice against the most numerous of them all; the so-called cabbage whites, a vernacular name which lumps together large whites, small whites, green-veined whites and probably wood whites too were they less rare. This habit implies that the caterpillars of them all eat cabbages which is wrong; the only ones which do significant damage are the large whites and their females, having laid their eggs, obligingly leave behind a scent which deters others from laying on the same leaf. This poses the question as to why no-one has produced a spray for cabbage-growing gardeners to use which replicates this scent.

Amongst the throng each day around our buddleias a minor drama was played out. The stars of the show were a small tortoiseshell, evidently a male and extremely tatty, and a comely freshly-hatched peacock with which it fell in love. A one-way courtship lasted several days and consisted of spiral flights interspersed with sessions on the flower-heads when the tortoiseshell would snuggle up behind the larger peacock and flutter his wings as if fanning irresistible aphrodisiac scents over her. This is a common tactic amongst butterflies wishing to push things along, but one which now went unnoticed by the peacock. Eventually the tortoiseshell gave up and disappeared but the episode reminded me of a time when, as a child, I had tried to cross these same two species, the rationale being that as they had matching life-cycles and the caterpillars of both ate nettles, all I had to do was put them together in a cage with nettles and nature would take its course. After all I had a book with a picture of an odd looking tortoiseshell which I, at the age of eight, imagined was the outcome of just such a coupling. But this was not so; this tortoiseshell was one which, in its pupal stage, had been injured by excessive heat, something which happens quite often and the resulting aberrations are sufficiently consistent to feature in books. Cross-breeds are another matter altogether and seldom occur. So both my experiment and the overtures of the lovelorn tortoiseshell came to nothing.

Word that, in this suddenly perfect summer, purple emperors were still flying in early August up on Bignor Hill sent us scuttling off to see what we could find. No purple emperors that day but plenty of others, all enjoying warm sunshine. Chief amongst them were silver-washed fritillaries. Three weeks earlier we had seen the first of these in Ebernoe woods but that day only the males had hatched and they were busy marking out territories, fighting off intruders and watching for hatching females. Once these hatch there are endless flirtatious games of catch-me-if-you-can played out sometimes amongst the tree-tops and sometimes along the woodland rides. Mated females then retire to the shade to lay their eggs in the crevices of tree bark, carefully choosing a place where, next spring, the hatching caterpillars can easily reach the dog violets upon which they feed.

By now, though, all work was done and the urgencies of youth had subsided. Time now for a leisurely get-together, flitting around in the sun amongst the flower-heads of hemp agrimony and thistle. Silver-washed fritillaries are amongst the largest and most stately of our indigenous butterflies and to be with so many in a remote downland wood brought its own special pleasure. It was only later that we heard that also there, but unseen by us, were some of the rare form *Valezina*. These are females with a rare recessive gene which results in the normal rich chestnut background being replaced by a soft olive green... beauty indeed. Despite a life-time of consorting with butterflies I have still to meet *Valezina*.

October 2013

Epic journeys

Animals of all shapes and sizes are constantly moving around looking for places to feed and breed, and because birds are so easy to see they are the ones that attract the most attention. A crescendo is reached each autumn when an estimated 2 billion passerines, 2.5 million wildfowl, 2 million raptors and untold millions of waders migrate from the Eurasian Arctic to spend the winter in Africa. Huge as these numbers are, they represent just a small proportion of what amounts to a massive and almost continuous world-wide movement of bird populations buried within which are some journeys of truly epic proportions. Consider, for example, the challenge faced by a Siberian-born willow warbler which flies every year of its life from its birth-place to Southern Africa and back, a round trip of nearly 7,500 miles. Staggering as this may be, at least this tiny bird flies for the most part over land, so can stop to rest and feed along the way. But not so the black-tailed godwits which fly with fast, energy-consuming wing beats from Alaska to New Zealand, a non-stop journey of 7000 miles across the vast expanse of the Pacific Ocean; much the same as an Olympic sprinter running a marathon without drink or food, flat out all the way.

Then there are arctic terns (so similar in looks to common terns that confused twitchers, have invented the all-embracing name "commic tern") that spend 9 months each year commuting between the Antarctic and the Arctic. Thus it was that an arctic tern fledgling ringed on the Farne Islands off the coast of Northumberland was found three months later near Melbourne, Australia. Shearwaters, likewise, are small birds with slender wings that spend most of their lives skimming the waves far out to sea. Some have been tracked flying up to 45,000 miles per year so that a bird which lives for 30 years, and many do, would have flown the equivalent of 50 circuits of our planet. The only time they come to land is to nest down burrows, usually on rat-free islands. Like puffins they return each year to exactly the same burrow where they meet up again with the same mate as the previous year whom they may not have seen for six months. So strong is this homing instinct that a shearwater removed from its burrow on an island off the coast of Pembroke and taken by plane to Boston, Massachusetts, 3100 miles away where it was released, was back home in the same burrow just ten days later. Albatrosses are another bird famed for their ability to fly immense distances by gently gliding low over water. To do this they have evolved slender wings with a 10 foot span which use the up-draft from the waves to keep them airborne. So specialised are they that an albatross must first gain speed by running over the surface before it can take off; and when it lands it does so with an undignified flop. It is an interesting fact that the structure of these wings were closely studied by the engineers who designed the un-manned drones that are so controversially used in modern warfare.

Another peripatetic bird that is better known to us here is the swift which famously sleeps whilst flying. Thus a swift with young to feed say here in Fittleworth is able, when times are hard, to make day-trips using thermal currents to forage for food in places as far away as northern Germany. Another epic journey but of an entirely different nature is that undertaken by a particular species of dung beetle. This insect constructs a ball of dung 1,141 times its own weight. It then rolls its load (equivalent in human terms to the weight of six double-decker buses each full of people) several hundred yards over difficult, often hilly, terrain to reach its hole. Dung beetles are one of only two animal species that use the Milky Way as an aid to navigation. We are the other.

Birds on the move face many hazards of which hunger and exhaustion are the most obvious. Just two examples illustrate the sort of risks taken; black-necked cranes fly from Tibet to Bhutan high over the Himalayas and whooper swans have been measured at altitudes of 27000 feet in temperatures of minus 40°c. Evan so, the sad fact is that we humans add hugely to their problems. For instance, in north-east India, hunters kill an estimated 140,000 migrating birds each year. Add to this the fact that one in five of the geese coming down from Siberia to over-winter at the Wildfowl and Wetland Trust Reserve at Slimbridge on the Severn Estuary are found to have gun-shot wounds. In both these examples it might be said in mitigation that these hunters are simply providing the food necessary for the survival of their families. But not so others, especially those in the Mediterranean countries where the tradition of shooting, netting and liming for migrating song-birds takes a massive toll each year and provides at best no more than small gourmet titbits for those already adequately fed.

No round-up such as this is complete without a mention of European eels. Hatched as elvers in the Sargasso Sea near Bermuda, they perform one of nature's greatest feats by swimming 3,500 miles across the Atlantic to enter the fresh-water rivers and lakes of Europe. There they live and grow for the next twenty years before returning to the Sargasso Sea to lay eggs and start the whole process all over again. And - even more extraordinary - the next generation of elvers always return to exactly the same European waters that were previously home to their parents. This inflexible routine, though, exposes them to the danger of unexpected obstructions getting in their way. It is heart-warming, therefore, to read of a recent mission of mercy undertaken by the Environment Agency in Somerset who discovered that the recent construction of dams along the river Yoe were blocking the passage of elvers inexorably swimming up-river to their traditional family lake. So they laid on tankers to transport them by road for the final twenty miles of their epic Odyssey.

November 2013

Nature Matters

Special times spent amongst birds

It was late in June and at long last there was some real warmth in the sun. We were walking along a cliff-top in North Cornwall. Larks were singing and stonechats seemed to dart out of every gorse bush we passed. And best of all, word was that choughs had been nesting in the area, although the local expert who served us in the local Farm Shop had told us that he himself had not seen them for a couple of weeks and feared that by now they may have dispersed. These birds, whose name rhymes with "toughs", are members of the crow family. A little larger than a jackdaw, they have longish, down-curved red beaks and red legs. They nest amongst rocky coastal cliffs and whenever I have seen them they seem to have taken on something of the wild beauty of these places. Having once been widely distributed in Britain they are now confined to just a few places in Pembrokeshire, the Hebrides and western Ireland. So there was understandable excitement amongst birders when, about ten years ago, choughs returned to a former stronghold near The Lizard in Cornwall. It was, therefore, good to hear that they had spread to the headlands near Plastow even if, as it turned out, we were too late to see them ourselves.

Our path along the top took us close to a stack of rock which rose straight up out of the sea so that the top was level with us and only about twenty yards off the cliff-edge. At one end of this was a lone herring gull with two fluffy chicks and at the other a group of about ten adults, constantly flapping their wings and calling to others on a nearby ledge. Gulls these days are becoming increasingly common inland where they tend to congregate and squabble noisily over scraps in places where they are not always welcome. As a consequence they are vilified as scavengers and pests. But back here, where nature intended them to be, amongst rocks spattered with patches of golden lichen, clumps of thrift and bush-like red-flowered tree mallow, they were transformed once more into birds of power and beauty. Even their cries, which sound so raucous around a council tip, here further enhanced a beautifully natural scene.

Each time the tide comes in over mudflats it drives before it an assortment of waders and sea duck. And in winter when their numbers are increased a thousand-fold by all the birds that come down from their breeding grounds in the Arctic, the spectacle is unforgettable. A good place to see all this is on the Wash where the RSPB have an ideally situated reserve at Snettisham near Hunstanton. It is an isolated area involving a long walk to reach the ideal spot but has several virtues. One is that the wide array of wader species that spend the winter there include knots. These are medium-sized, short-billed waders that stay in tight flocks so that on the ground at a distance they resemble a solid dark carpet and it needs powerful binoculars to see that this mass is actually a mosaic of thousands of individual birds. And in flight its as if they were a dense cloud of drifting smoke which constantly changes shape and direction. Combined with this is the ability of a flock of several hundred knots to twist and turn in exact unison so that an attacker is confronted first by a sea of brown backs and then by one of white bellies. The effect is much like flashing tinsel and as a result predators even as adroit as peregrine falcons are bamboozled and give up. As the tide comes in so the knots rise in a cloud, wheel around and then, as one, drop down again. At Snettisham the tide comes in over several miles and every time the knots take wing thousands of other shore birds get caught up in the general excitement and so the air is constantly full of circling flocks of oystercatchers, godwits, curlew and a myriad assortment of smaller waders. Meanwhile shelduck, wigeon and goldeneye rest on the water until descending darkness compels them too to rise up in small fast-flying flocks.

A second feature at Snettisham is that it sits nicely on the route taken by pink-footed geese that have spent the day grazing on farmland to the north-east and at sundown fly in over the mudflats seeking the night-time sanctuary of the flooded gravel pits behind the sea-wall where they are safe from marauding foxes. These pits are man-made and provide little islands where birds can roost at night and, in spring, is used by nesting turns. But in the winter the geese come in at sundown and return to graze again at dawn. In the air, honking as they go, they are a captivating sight. So if high-tide coincides with dawn or dusk then the magic of waders driven in by the tide and the geese flying overhead coincides. And those lucky enough to be there on such an occasion will witness what many have described as the best wild-life spectacle these islands have to offer. And such it was on an evening in mid-October when we were there.

They say that a little later in the winter when the tide is at its highest there may be up to 100,000 knots instead of the estimated 50,000 we saw. And they also say that by January the geese will be coming over in skeins of hundreds instead of the twenties and thirties we saw. But who cares – to attempt to judge such an event by counting the birds would be as meaningless as rating a piece of music by the number of notes. And anyway we had the bonus that after a week of overcast skies, the day of our visit had been bright and sunny, so that our bird saga was played out against the backdrop of a sunset which lit up sky and water like no other. And to cap it all, as the sun sank over the horizon so it was replaced by a bright full moon across which, just as we left for home, a skein of pink-footed geese flew in perfect formation.

December 2013

How important is knowing the name?

Anyone who has ever looked out of a window or up at the sky knows a thing or two about birds. Who doesn't notice the brisk purpose of a sparrow, the airy insouciance of a gull or the dramatic power of a hawk? Birds are beautiful, you can encounter them anywhere and they embody one of the primeval human aspirations; flight.

These words come from a book called *How to be a (bad) Birdwatcher* by Simon Barnes. His theme throughout aims to reassure those of us who cannot put a name to every bird we see by reminding us that there is still plenty left to enjoy, just by being amongst them in the places where they live. Indeed last month these notes attempted to describe the feeling of awe that comes from being amongst a huge mass of water-birds when they move from their feeding grounds to their night-time roosts. Implicit in that account was that even if the observer did not know the names of any of the participating birds, the experience of just being there would be sufficient to fill anyone with a sense of wonderment. After all, poets, artists and musicians have, down the ages, drawn inspiration from the natural world.

So why do so many of us spend so much time trying to put a name to everything we see? Well, animal life excites our curiosity and there is no doubting that an extra level of pleasure is to be had from knowing a bit more about whatever it is we have just seen; what is it doing, why is it there and so on. And to get the answers means going to a book, finding the name and reading what it says. For example, when watching that evening flight (described last month) there was extra enjoyment in knowing that the geese coming in over the water were winter visitors which had arrived on the Wash in September. Many had started from far-off Greenland, but had been joined by others as they passed through Iceland. These same geese had been coming there all their lives and will return home in March to raise families. Next winter they will return with their new offspring in a timeless rhythm which has endured for centuries. But to acquire this information we must first know their name; pink-footed geese. Then we can read about the rest and sprinkle the occasion with a little extra magic.

But identification can, on occasion, be a problem as I know only too well from trying to sort out spring warblers or spot a little stint amongst a flock of dunlin darting in and out of the water along a shoreline. Many respected naturalists rely on what they call jizz, a term which covers often indefinable features which they know beyond doubt is unique to a particular species; rather as a man might instantly identify his wife without the need to refer to such details as eye-colour, call-note or gait. But over-reliance to jizz can lead to lazy habits. Consider, for example, the birder who relies solely on this to identify a curlew; understandable in a way because a curlew is a pretty unique bird. But what if it is in a place where size is hard to judge? What if, in reality it is the much rarer but smaller whimbrel and the observer has over-looked the need to check for the give-away eye-stripe which distinguishes the latter? He or she will have missed the opportunity of a highly-prized tick on the day's list of sightings and with it bragging rights in the pub later.

Jizz, on the other hand, is probably sufficient to identify most of the butterflies likely to be seen in this country. But first it is helpful to know what you might expect to see in the habitat you are visiting at that particular time of the year. By so doing the field is narrowed down to just a handful of species and this enables you to anticipate in advance any where jizz alone will be insufficient for identification. Two such species which share both habitat and flight seasons and, from a jizz perspective, look much the same are small skippers and Essex skippers. Separating them, however, demands effort; first you must manoeuvre into a position from which you can see the underside of the antennae and since skippers always perch near to the ground, this often requires the skill of a limbo dancer. Once in position you must look upwards to see a small spot at the tip and on the underside of the antennae. If this is black you have found an Essex skipper and if red a small skipper. Or you may elect not to bother and instead be content to be in a nice place on a nice day and simply enjoy watching pretty little chestnut brown butterflies flitting around amongst spring flowers. And why not?

So far this winter the traffic around our bird-feeders has been much lighter than usual. At first I thought that a mild autumn might have provided the birds with all they needed in the wild. But I am now worried that the wretched spring in 2013 may have made raising families difficult and thus there are simply fewer around. As winter weather takes a hold we shall find out and in the meantime large flocks of winter visitors from Scandinavia such as redwing and fieldfare roam the countryside searching for berries. Along with them have come wood pigeons and chaffinches to swell our own resident populations. Visiting chaffinches do not integrate with ours, instead remaining in flocks that feed in arable fields and beech woods. They are slightly larger and the males a bit pinker than resident birds and their flocks sometimes contain a few of the closely related but much more colourful bramblings. An interesting thing about these visitors is that the females greatly out-number the males, so much so that flocks going to Ireland are composed almost entirely of females. And finally, special excitement from Waltham wildbrooks where two great grey shrikes and five ravens stayed for several days in November. But no sign yet of last year's favourite; waxwings.

January 2014

Wildlife and the weather

Street traders in New York are famous for the speed with which they can switch their merchandise according to the needs of the moment; umbrellas when it rains and dark glasses the minute the sun comes out. Having regard to our fluctuating weather it might be useful for wild animals to learn the same trick. Arguments persist as to what precisely is causing global climate to change but the impact is becoming ever more apparent; something is causing the polar ice-caps to melt with knock effects which extend far beyond the discomfort of polar bears. Something which may or may not be a direct result of this is the succession of extremes in unseasonable weather which put huge pressure on all living things, not least us. A few things that went on through 2013 serve as examples.

Sea-birds of the auk family remain far out in the ocean all winter, gathering in spring in huge numbers at coastal nesting sites where the sand-eels upon which they feed their young abound. Until recently these colonies were well-established all round the British Isles, across to Scandinavia and up to Iceland. In recent years, however, ocean currents have changed course with the result that sand-eels have all but disappeared in the northerly regions (helped, it has to be said, by pirate fishing) but are still plentiful down south. As a result the northern colonies have declined, some drastically, and those in the south have flourished.

Insects which have extended their range northward across the Channel in response to our milder winters sometimes make the news, specially when they provide an opportunity for scary headlines about bees with deadly stings and giant ladybirds which shoulder out our own indigenous species. The reality is seldom anything like this. The bee, incidentally, after ten years amongst us has turned out to be much more docile than many of our native bees (unless unreasonably provoked) and by last summer had spread north to Scotland. And as for the ladybird, yes it does seem to be a better survivor than our native ladybirds but we should perhaps remember that the evolution of all species has been driven by a need to adapt to circumstances, a process that ensures that it is the ones best suited to conditions that survive. Were it not so we ourselves would not be here.

Other arrivals from the Continent last summer included several species of moth and long-tailed blue butterflies. As recently as forty years ago these little butterflies were unable to survive winters much north of the Mediterranean rim. Since then there has been the odd sighting this side of the Channel but in 2013 for the first time females were seen laying eggs here. If these hatch successfully and long-tailed blues are added to our list of resident butterflies it will provide us with the best example we have of a phenomenon known as "back-to-front" mimicry. This describes the device whereby a butterfly tricks a predator into thinking that its rear-end is its head, thereby deflecting any attack to a part of its body where it will not be fatal. It is achieved by having tails at the base of the hind wings which resemble tiny antennae, reinforced by spots on the wings which look like eyes. This might not fool you and me but it must work sometimes otherwise it would never have evolved into standard kit. Several of our blues and hairstreaks also use the ploy but in none is it so well-developed as with these little gems.

The story of 2013 as a whole was of extremes; January, dull with snow, followed by a March which was the coldest since 1962. The rest of spring (except, happily, the two days allotted to our Village Garden Trail) was cold and miserable so that nesting birds had a rough time finding food for their young, bees necessary to pollinate spring blossom were scarce and butterflies were all but invisible. Then in July the sun suddenly came out and remained shining more or less continuously until early September. Spring butterflies which should have been finished by July came from no-where to join the normal mid-summer broods of peacocks, red admirals, commas and brimstones. So too small tortoiseshells some of which were so smart that they were obviously newly hatched and others scruffy enough to suggest that they had lived through an extended hibernation begun the previous autumn. And just to complete the happy scene there came a mass of migrants from across the Channel including clouded yellows, painted ladies, and even the occasional much rarer Queen of Spain fritillary and swallowtail.

Then it all ended and we drifted through a bright but late autumn with mild weather. Red admirals and a peacock were feeding on our arbutus whenever the sun shone and did so until just before Christmas. Then came the gales, rain and devastating floods. Against the background of human suffering these wrought it seems heartless to mention that wildlife also suffered. But in the context of these notes perhaps just one word will suffice; for every field flooded there will have been untold numbers of small mammals drowned, with adverse consequences also for their predators further up the food-chain Yet through it all westerly winds have given us a mild winter; sufficiently so to enable a Mr Gaskin to write telling us that on 3rd January skylarks were singing from a clear blue sky in a blustery North Yorkshire. And here in Sussex in the annual rush to be the first to see a new year butterfly, both small tortoiseshells and peacocks were reported by 6th January. Doubtless, each of us has his or her own favourite "first signs of spring" be it snow drops, the smell of fresh-mown grass or woodpeckers tapping out messages of love to one another on tree-trunks. But here is one that has the added attraction of having come via the Sussex Record Office from the hand-written records kept by the Parham Estate gamekeeper, Henry Floate. Written in 1872, his notes tell us that on the Estate heronry the birds start to build their nests in about the third week in January – a sure sign that spring is in the air – nipping in to steal twigs from neighbouring rookeries before the rooks had returned to guard them.

February 2014

Nature Matters

More storms and a tale from Mongolia

It is just about possible as I write to remember that in the early days of January there was a brief period of calm between storms, sufficient to allow the papers to report weather so mild that snowdrops were flowering, birds nesting, swallows arriving and butterflies flying. The inference was that, despite everything, spring had got off to an early start, a view that overlooked the fact that because all living things have evolved side by side many life-forms are inter-depend ven if only as a source of food. Consider, for instance, a bird that normally nests in April and has grown to rely upon newly hatched caterpillars to feed its young; what does it do if faced with a brood to feed in the barren month of January? It's the same with butterflies that come out of hibernation before the flowers that provide nectar are in bloom – and swallows zooming around in cold January air trying to catch non-existent airborn insects to sustain themselves. As it turned out, of course, incessant rain and wind returned, so it might be worth looking elsewhere to see what this erratic weather is doing to our wildlife. Surprisingly over the past 40 years average annual temperatures, recorded in Eastbourne, have risen by just 1.3°c; not much but enough to have influenced the distribution of some familiar wildlife species. The pattern has been to shift everything to the north. Thus birds, insects and even flowers previously confined to southern Europe are coming north and a few have established themselves here. Concurrently winter-visiting birds from the sub-Arctic are now remaining further north than in the past. There are enough of these to have earned the collective name "short stoppers".

Now for something a little different. It concerns a man called Jimmy, the son of an oil company executive whose job involved frequent overseas postings. As a consequence Jimmy's childhood had been spent amongst people of different backgrounds and cultures, and the experience had fired a curiosity that lasted into adulthood. As a child he had taken photographs and this had lead to a career in commercial photography but his burning desire became one of creating a pictorial record of the world's remotest tribes before they were swallowed up by the ever-invasive outside world. A chance meeting with a wealthy Dutchman who agreed to finance him had cleared the way, so off he went. Jimmy knew that he would be entering a world of isolated people with traditions and rituals of their own and with little understanding of where he had come from or what he wanted. There would be no shared language and gaining their trust would therefore be both difficult and vital.

The book* that Jimmy later wrote describes just one way in which the barriers of suspicion were overcome. His hosts on that occasion were the Kazakhs, a semi-nomadic Turkic tribe living in outer Mongolia with beliefs derived from various pre-Islamic cults. They raise sheep, camels and horses for food and clothing and their men-folk practise an ancient tradition hunting by flying golden eagles from horse-back at prey high up in the hills. Jimmy's arrival amongst them was accepted with cool indifference and several days passed without any sign of the level of trust or cooperation which he needed. So he tried a new tack; he decided to join his hosts in their evening ritual, drinking the local spirit. But Jimmy, unaccustomed to such things, quickly keeled over and fell asleep. Some hours later he was woken by the urgent call of nature and, not wishing to disturb the rest, all now comatose close by, he rolled himself slowly to the edge of the tent, lifted a flap and, still prone, did the necessary. Not many minutes later as he drifting back to sleep there came a thundering noise from outside. Unknown to him, Jimmy had laid a scent that had attracted the local reindeer and in their rush to lick the places that Jimmy had enriched with vital salts they brought down the side of the tent. The ensuing commotion brought everyone to their feet and when they noticed that Jimmy himself was the centre of the reindeer's attention they realised what had happened. The mood immediately changed, everyone burst out laughing, the damaged tent was repaired and the bottles re-appeared. And crucially Jimmy's heroics had won him the place amongst them that he craved.

Next morning as the sun rose the hunters were ready mounted with eagles resting on their arms waiting for Jimmy to join them. Together they trekked up into the hills to a place that Jimmy had previously identified as perfect for his photography and the hunters patiently took up the positions requested of them. Finally he removed his gloves to take the photo and immediately his fingers froze to the point of being useless. Partly from pain and partly from frustration, tears came into his eyes and he turned his head to hide his grief. It was only then that he saw that two women had followed them up into the hills and were now approaching him. One took his hands in hers and, opening her fur-cape, held them close within whilst the other enveloped him from behind. They held him thus for perhaps five minutes, all the time gently humming against the howling wind as would a mother comforting a loved-one in need. When he was restored Jimmy turned back to the hunters half-expecting to see that they had abandoned him and gone about their business. But not so. They had held their positions to perfection, heavy eagles resting high on their arms waiting for their ladies to do what had to be done.

And so Jimmy got the photograph of his dreams. "These people did not understand what I wanted or why" he later wrote, "but they felt exactly how much I needed it and gave themselves to me accordingly".

March 2014

* *Before they pass away*, by Jimmy Nelson. The picture Jimmy took, and others, can be seen on the Amazon website.

Thoughts for April

Spring is a time of change so it is a good time to take a look at what is happening in the countryside. Bees, hoverflies and butterflies are coming out of hibernation and birds move about with a new sense of urgency, sorting out mates, establishing territories and building nests. Some birds mate for life and remain close together all year round. Others mate for life but separate each year after raising a family, spending the rest of the year apart. Each spring they return to the same nest-site where the bond is renewed and together they raise another family. This pattern of behaviour is prevalent amongst migrants so that often the paired birds have often spent up to nine months of the year many hundreds of miles apart. Other birds are monogamous for the duration of just one breeding season, finding new mates each year. And finally there is a group that takes promiscuity to a new level where the young in any given nest could each have been fathered by any one of several local males. And just to take the merry confusion one step further the females often take the opportunity of laying their eggs in the nests of neighbours should the rightful owner be absent. At the risk of straying into the language of anthropomorphism it must be said that the birds most guilty of this wanton conduct are frequently those which we humans look upon as the most demure and loveable.

Parental duties such as nest-building, incubation and the feeding of young are shared in different proportions according to the species. Female kestrels stand at one extreme, seldom leaving the nest once the first egg is laid so that all food both for her and the young are caught and brought to the nest by the male. This is an arduous task, the more so since the kestrel's most usual method of catching food by hovering and diving to the ground uses a great deal of the bird's energy. As a consequence it is not unusual for a male kestrel to wear itself to a frazzle in fulfilling these duties. But as an example of masculine devotion to parental duty kestrels come a poor second to red-necked phalaropes, lovely little birds the size of a moorhen but better looking. They breed in the tundra, but sadly only occasionally come here as passage migrants. With these birds role reversal is so complete that the male attends to all incubation, feeding and subsequent nursery-work. The female even takes the initiative in matters relating to courtship and mating, even to the extent of having the more colourful plumage. When ready she drops her eggs on bare ground and that's it; she takes no further part in family life other than paying an occasional short visit just to ensure that the male is seeing to things in a proper manner. In due course the eggs hatch into chicks that swim from birth, their father, in sole charge, clucking around as would a mother duck. Remember, too, that unless the downy chicks have physical contact with the adult that is close enough to ensure that a coating of oil from his feathers cover them, they, the chicks, will become water-logged and die of cold. I once watched several families of these fascinating birds swimming around on a lake in Iceland, each attended by its father. The females, in other words presumably the mothers, were also thereabouts but none paid the slightest attention to the comings and goings of these family groups.

It would be a big surprise if our wildlife is not affected in some way by a winter during which vast tracts of our countryside was flooded, gales raged but also one that was unusually mild. Ground-dwelling mammals will have suffered, either by drowning or by being unable to find food and this will have had consequential effects upon birds and larger mammals that prey upon them. When the water-meadows to the south of the village were flooded greylag and Canada geese and small flocks of wigeon moved in along with herons, shovelers, (duck with outsize beaks for scooping up surface food), three distinct families of mute swans and even a black swan, the last almost certainly one of the feral birds normally swimming around on Benbow Pond near Easebourne. These birds had moved there to find food and there was no reason to think that they had suffered anything more serious than temporary dislocation.

On the other hand for butterflies the generally mild winter poses unexpected threats. They arise from the need for butterflies in northern Europe to spend the winter hibernating, a process wherein they hide away and shut down all body processes except those vital to staying alive. Butterflies can hibernate in any one of the four stages in their life-cycle according to species and in each are protected from extreme cold by producing proteins that prevent their body fluids from freezing. Mild weather, on the other hand, results in the formation of pathogens that lead to disease. Mild weather also carries the risk that they come out of hibernation when their bodies are still in a state of semi-torpor and before there is nectar to provide vital food. And, lastly, a mild winter will undoubtedly have seen an increase in a butterfly's natural predators. These include all the vicious little solitary wasps that have the delightful habit of laying their eggs directly into the bodies of caterpillars. This way they ensure that the hatching grubs have readily at hand an ample supply of fresh food.

And finally something different to ponder; there are more living organisms in a table-spoonful of soil than there are people on planet Earth. And if you don't believe this I simply quote wording on a box that contains a small microscope produced by the Natural History Museum in London and sold in their own shop. It is not, I promise, Nature Matters idea of an April Fool hoax!!
April 2014

Nature Matters

Garden birds; winners & losers

Like all wild animals, birds have two essential needs: food and somewhere safe to live and raise a family and to meet these challenges throughout the changing seasons there is continuous movement. Birds in Sussex can choose from a wide range of habitats but because three quarters of our county is devoted to farmland changes in farming practices bear particularly heavily upon them and this is a factor to be borne in mind when reading the results of the RSPB Big Garden Birdwatch. This is a nationwide survey conducted annually during the last week-end in January and is now in its 35th year. Members of the public are invited to record and send in the names of any birds seen in their garden over just those two days. They need not belong to the RSPB.

This year's survey tells us amongst other things that the number of robins recorded has declined over 35 years by 45%, that chaffinches have declined by 50%, house sparrows by 62% and thrushes by 81%. Winners have been magpies, crows and collared doves with garden sightings of each at least doubling. However nothing compares with the massive 743% increase in woodpigeons, a bird that RSPB says benefits from the modern tendency for farmers to sow more winter crops. These trends are broadly in line with the findings surveys that cover a wider base than just gardens, except that they seem to overstate the magnitude of the declines.

A couple of points worth noting are, first, that the birds showing the largest declines are the ones that might be expected to have benefited the most from the increasing use of garden bird feeders. To see how large a factor this is, we need look no further than the amount of space given over to bird feeding equipment in any garden centre, and the fact that the reverse is the case might seem to support those who say that by encouraging birds to congregate in one place we set them up as easy targets for the likes of sparrow hawks. But predators take their food wherever they can find it and if it is not available around a bird table they simply go elsewhere. More important is that bird feeders and adjacent areas, unless kept scrupulously clean, can quickly become a source of disease, especially in damp weather. An example is provided by greenfinches the numbers of which fell recently by 25% in just one year. The killer was a virus that was transmitted by the bird's saliva so that bird feeders were contaminated and nestlings taking food from infected parents also perished.

Another factor that may have distorted the records is the recent sequence of mild winters which have made it possible for birds to find all the food they need in the wild without the need to come to garden feeders. This was evident in our garden last winter when several species of birds that in the past were frequent visitors to our feeders were either completely absent or much reduced. Others in the village with feeders have had varying experiences extending on one occasion to a blackcap that dropped in on Pauline and Quinton Gilpin in Greatpin Croft. And in another garden nearby goldfinches were regular visitors all winter.

These are minor caveats and should not obscure two huge benefits coming out of this survey. The first is that, because it is conducted at the same time each year and has run for 35 years trends have meaning. And the second is simply that no less than half-million people up and down the country were prepared to sit in their gardens for an hour over a chilly week-end in January, identify and write down the names of every bird they saw, and then take the trouble to send their lists in to the RSPB. Amazing!! And perhaps there were some who, in the process, have forged friendships with some of the birds they saw similar to the one we have, by chance, established with a robin.

It all started two years ago when I was to sitting by our front gate waiting to greet visitors to the annual garden trail. It was cold and wet, guests were thin on the ground and I was wondering how I would pass the time. Soon, though, I was joined by a fledgling robin, too young to fly and looking a bit lost. Glad of the company, I went in to fetch it some food and as a result we passed a pleasant afternoon together. Thus started an enduring relationship and now whenever we go outside this robin appears from nowhere and hops around close by in the hope of getting some food. Now, as I write these notes, she is busy tending a family of four nestlings in our garage, quite unperturbed by being in the midst of our daily comings and goings. And this simple bond of trust between a wild bird and us human beings provides more pleasure than would seeing any number of rarities, here only by the accident of a freak wind. So perhaps, by engaging the attention of half a million people, the Big Garden Birdwatch has enabled some of them to enjoy this same pleasure. If so, the RSPB will have fulfilled what should surely be one of their most important roles.

May 2014

Birds of prey

Most birds of prey are carnivores, living by catching, killing and tearing the flesh off their prey. As a consequence they have developed large talons, hooked beaks and a persona that radiates ferocity. Buzzards are the species most often seen around here and it is hard to remember that only ten years ago these majestic birds were still confined to the west country where word was that high density was adversely effecting breeding success. Thus expanding their range was a matter of survival and buzzards have now taken over from kestrels as Britain's most numerous birds of prey, their soaring flight, eagle-like silhouette and mewing call bringing new delights to the countryside. Indeed this resemblance to a small eagle is often used by those Scots who are ever-keen to put one over visiting Sassenachs; all they do is point to a buzzard and tell us that it is a golden eagle and that custom demands that we now buy everyone a dram to celebrate the sighting. A variant on this theme occurred a couple of years ago when it was reported on the internet that a golden eagle had been seen near Hove. Local birders immediately jumped in to say that as these birds were unknown in Sussex it must have been a buzzard. The observer replied that he was a visitor from the Hebrides where he was the RSPB warden with several golden eagle eyries on his patch. He was therefore well qualified, he said, to tell a golden eagle from a buzzard. The Hove eagle, incidentally, stayed long enough to thrill many Sussex birders before moving on into Hampshire.

Buzzards often perch on posts on the look-out for prey, a hunting technique which avoids the irritation of being mobbed by rooks and others. They feed mostly on rabbits and small mammals and can often be seen foraging on the ground for worms and beetles. In spring and autumn they are sometimes joined by their near-relatives, honey buzzards, passing through on passage. The two species look very much alike but honey buzzards specialise in catching and eating bees from which, showing extraordinary dexterity, they first extract the sting.

Red kites are another large raptor recently arrived here in Sussex. They are not yet as plentiful as buzzards from which they can be distinguished by their long, deeply forked tails, red colour and languid flight. Once a common sight across the country, they were persecuted a century ago before being rescued from oblivion by conservationists. Those around here come from a colony introduced into the Chilterns several years ago. Kites feed by scavenging or catching small mammals. Marsh harriers are another large raptor increasingly seen in winter or on passage, the occasional pair remaining here to breed. Both hen harriers and ospreys pass through on passage. Two falcons here all year are kestrels that hover head into the wind, pouncing on small mammals, and peregrines that catch other birds by diving (stooping) from high up at speeds of up 180 mph. They are said to be, pound-for-pound, the most efficient killing animals on the planet (excluding us). In summer they are joined by hobbies, so agile that they catch and eat swifts on the wing, and in winter by merlins, no larger than a mistle thrush. And finally two hawks, both with the ability to chase down small birds by dodging in and out between dense trees. One is the frequently-seen sparrow hawk and the other the larger goshawk, a bird so eagerly sort by egg collectors and falconers that any information concerning its whereabouts is strictly secret. There is reported to be just one pair breeding "somewhere" in Sussex.

Which brings us to owls, birds so idiosyncratic that the Greeks accorded them God-like status. Shakespeare, too, frequently taps in to popular superstitions associated with owls to add mood and menace to his writings and Edward Lear, master of the whimsy, had an owl and a pussycat going to sea in a beautiful pea-green boat. But to birders owls are just birds of prey, hunting either exclusively at night or sometimes also by day. For a long time it was thought that their nearest relatives were nightjars but recent advances in genetic analysis suggest that they are directly related to diurnal raptors and have simply evolved physical features that better equip them for hunting in low light. These special features include exceptional binocular vision, disc-shaped faces surrounded by feathers that reflect sound back into highly efficient ears and soft feathers that ensure flight so quiet that it is inaudible to its victims. The extent to which these features have developed relates directly to the life-style adopted by each owl species. But with all of them the importance of eyesight is paramount, as demonstrated by the proportion of the skull that is occupied by the organs of sight. In humans this never exceeds 5% and in birds other than owls it is about 50%. But with owls a massive 70% of the skull is occupied by eyes. If we were similarly equipped our skulls, re-shaped but with unchanged capacity, would have eyeballs the size of a large grapefruit.

Of those living around here barn owls fly in daylight and are therefore the ones most often seen. But the exceptionally cold spring last year robbed them of food and the national population fell by 71%. Short-eared owls come here in winter but it is tawny owls that are the most numerous. However they remain out of sight during the day so pass unnoticed. Small birds in a state of agitation often give away the presence of a hidden tawny owl. The picture here was taken on Fittleworth Common just before Easter. It is one of two tawny owlets that had fallen from their nest and were being fed by their parents.

June 2014

The secret lives of robins revealed

If robins were dogs they would be the kind that appear from nowhere, stand looking up at you, ears pricked and tails wagging, waiting to be given a biscuit - all of which conflicts with the fact that robins are aggressive little birds who spend a large part of their lives fighting. This paradox is well exemplified by experiments in which a pair of cock robins were placed in a cage containing a bowl of food over which they always squabbled. But when one of them hurt his leg on the side of the cage the other immediately drew back and began to comfort his injured foe with offers of food. A couple more stories are enough to confirm that robins are, indeed, unusual birds. The first comes from Birmingham where a man left his bedroom window open before going downstairs to have breakfast. When he returned he discovered that robins had started to build a nest in his bed which he left un-made for as long as they needed it. And the other relates to a pair in Walton Heath which built their nest in a wagon. Just after the eggs hatched, the wagon was required to go to Worthing and back. So one of the birds went with it, finding food for the young along the way.

But before delving further into the lives of these surprising birds, a word about their mentor, David Lack. Born in 1910, Lack spent his childhood in Norfolk where he had ample opportunity to indulge his love of nature. As a schoolboy he wrote several prize-winning essays that demonstrated a burgeoning interest in wildlife and in due course he went up to Cambridge to read Natural Science. In 1934 he set about the field-work that was to provide the basis for a ground-breaking monograph published in 1943 called *The Life of the Robin*. This book was the first to be written by a scientist from an ecological view-point; that is to say, based upon the subject's relationship with its environment. Interestingly he also sought to establish where possible a link between the characteristics of his subjects and ways in which these might benefit their survival. Lack was a committed Christian as well as a supporter of the Darwinian theory of evolution and he devoted a separate book to the reconciliation of these twin beliefs.

Lack spent the war working on the nation's radar defences which offered him a pre-view of how migrating birds would later be tracked. After the war his overriding interest in ecology rapidly put him at the forefront of a new wave of naturalists who took their scientific disciplines into the field and applied them to practical observation and it is a sad fact that the work of this generation coincided with the austerities of post-war Britain. He died aged only 63 in 1973 and as a consequence never got the public acclaim that came to later generations who could use the technology of modern film-making and television to bring both the science and the beauty of wildlife to a world-wide audience.

A review of a year in the life of a robin is best started in August by which time the season's breeding is done and it is time to moult. This involves the loss of flight feathers and is a time of peril. So they hide away in deep shrubbery until ready to re-appear in all their finery. That year's young now have red breasts and are fully charged up for lives as adults and there is much to be done. First they all separate out to find new territories, the sexes not yet sharing. Then in December the males begin to sing and the females abandon their territories to tour those of the males in search of partners they consider best fitted to father their future off-spring. But lady-robins are hard to please and as many as a fifth of the males are discarded as unfit for purpose, dissatisfied females preferring to look again at the paired males hoping to find one or two prepared to do a double shift. Such manoeuvres ensure that only the best genes are passed on to the next generation. These matters completed (more or less), the next two months are spent fine-tuning marital arrangements and bickering over territories. Then in March the rituals of courtship start up. This stimulates the females to build a nest, the pairs to mate and eggs to be laid. During incubation the male feeds the female on the nest or by calling off. But after the eggs hatch both parents feed the young. However soon the female starts to build a second nest and then the male takes sole charge of the young. From that point onwards, however, both parents begin to turn their attention to the new family, leaving the first lot to fend for themselves.

A couple of months ago I mentioned a robin that had become an honorary member of our family and was then sitting on eggs in our garage. Well, by the time the village Garden Trail came around they had become a family of five, all using the feeders at the back of our house. The young were quite capable of feeding themselves, but like teen-agers the world over were taking full advantage of over-indulgent parents. The scene was one of continuous activity, so I decided to set up a feeding station beside the gate where I would be greeting visitors on the trail. This way I could keep an eye on the birds and, as it turned out, provide a bit of a side-show for our guests. I suspected that the female was by then sitting on her second clutch of eggs not far away. Even so the young from the first brood were still hanging around intermittently being fed by their father. However over the two days of close observation the mood changed; squabbles became frequent and soon it seemed that the father was intent only on collecting food to take away. Thus my suspicion was strengthened; the nesting hen must be nearby and his duties now lay with her; as far as he was concerned the sooner the first lot shoved off the better. Confirmation came when finally the male came to the bowl, called and it was she, not the young, who came out from the nearby bushes. She perched on the rim opposite him, assumed a begging posture, opened her mouth and he, in a rather touching little scene, popped in some food, a gesture probably having more to do with pair-bonding than providing nourishment.

Since then the first brood have made their own way. And now, a couple of weeks on, the second brood have hatched and the parents are again bringing them food.

July 2014

A voyage to Norway and beyond

The unique geography of Norway makes it a hugely varied and interesting place for wildlife. The southern end lies on approximately the same latitude as northern Scotland and from there the mainland stretches on up north-east for a thousand miles, well into the Arctic Circle. And another 400 miles north across the Barents Sea lie the group of islands known to most of us as Spitzbergen but to the Norwegians as Svalbard. And 600 miles beyond that is the North Pole. More about Svalbard in a minute. First, though, a word about mainland Norway which consists of a coastal strip running the full length of the country backed by a magnificent range of mountains intersected by fjords. It is a rugged country with many habitations only accessible from the sea and as you move north so the land takes on the characteristics of pure Arctic tundra. Until about thirty years ago the economy was heavily dependent upon agriculture and fishing and indeed a feature of many of the small coastal towns are the number of fish-farms devoted to the rearing of salmon. However over the past 35 years North Sea oil has superseded all else and made Norway one of the world's most prosperous countries.

Superficially much of the habitat and therefore wildlife on offer in Norway might seem to replicate that of Scotland, especially the Western Highlands and Islands and indeed many interesting sea-birds and birds of the uplands are common to both places. However where Norway undoubtedly edges Scotland is that it offers a greater probability of seeing some of the favourites; white-tailed eagles, grey phalaropes, snow buntings, ptarmigan and so on. Add to this the possibility of a chance encounter with, say a gyr falcon or snowy owl and of course the numerous colonies of cliff-nesting birds such as puffins, guillemots little auks, kittiwakes and fulmars and you quickly have a birder's paradise.

Where Norway wins hands down, though, is with its range of mammals. Arctic foxes, pine martins and of course reindeer are common-place but nothing prepared us for the surprise of seeing half-a-dozen moose quietly grazing beside the road running out into the countryside from Tromso, a town just inside the Arctic Circle. Our guide told us that this would have been quite usual in mid-winter but not in summer when moose generally remain high up in the hills. Also high up in the hills and seldom seen are the lemmings, small rodents renowned for their mass migrations which often lead to fatal falls over the sides of cliffs. Marine mammals also attracted the attention of a group travelling with us from The Orca Society. Working tirelessly from a look-out in our bows of our ship this team recorded over 50 different species of whales, dolphins, porpoises and seals during the course of our 15 days at sea.

So now on to Svalbard, a place once used by the Russians for coal-mining but now reserved for scientific research and to a limited extent tourism.

However increasing pollution and despoliation by tourists has obliged the authorities to take further steps to protect a habitat so tender that just one human footprint on the damp tundra will do irreparable damage to the ground surface. Because of this it is obvious that visitors such as ourselves were (quite rightly) greatly restricted in both movement and numbers. As a consequence we were able to get little more than a broad perspective of the rugged grandeur of the landscape; distant views of the snow-covered mountains, deep valleys often encasing blue-tinted glaciers and lower down the fragile tundra with clumps of saxifrage, dwarf willow herb, lichens and mosses all in flower. And here and there, growing in a side-ways direction and to a height of just 3 inches, a tiny willow tree. It is amongst these delicate treasures that visitors were barred from wandering and although the reason was to be respected it would have been a huge shame to have travelled all that far if that were to be the limit of our experience.

But luck was with us in the shape of a fellow-passenger by the name of Ted Jackson. In 1970 Ted had worked with Peter Scott at Slimbridge and had been one of a five-man team sent to investigate the barnacle geese that spent each winter on the Solway Firth and were thought to breed on Svalbard. Scott's hunch at the time was that there existed three distinct races of barnacle geese, one that breeds on a group of islands in the high Russian Arctic called Novaya Zemlya and move through the Baltic to winter in Holland, another from Greenland that winter in Western Scotland and a third from Svalbard that winters on Solway Firth, and it was our very good fortune that 45 years on Ted Jackson was with us and able to give us an illustrated talk about his part in tracking the Svalbard birds.

The team had been cast off from a local mail ship with all their supplies in a small boat to scramble ashore on a little-known part of Svabard. Their first task was to locate the geese, set up camp and ensure their own safety from marauding polar bears. This done they required to work out a method of catching and ringing the geese. They discovered that shortly after the eggs hatched the adults went into a complete moult and for a short time were unable to fly. So they constructed a cage from drift-wood and discarded fishing nets and after much trial and error and over a period of several weeks succeeded in capturing and ringing a sufficient number of geese to serve their purpose. They were also assisted by the fact that the flock they were working on contained four leucistic birds, distinguished from the others by their lack of dark pigments. Remember that all this pioneering work was conducted before the advent of Satellite telephones and suchlike and the sense of isolation can only be imagined…..as can the sense of elation when, some months later, they visited the flocks of 35,000 or so barnacle geese now assembled for the winter on Solway Firth and there grazing quietly amongst them were the geese they had ringed on Svalbard along with all four leucistic birds.

August 2014

The charm of wagtails

For reasons that I will explain shortly I can still remember the first time I saw a wagtail in this country which was other than pied. It occurred long ago when our holidays were spent in Devon building sand castles, collecting cowrie shells and catching shrimps. The drive down from Surrey could be tedious and we had, over time, found a good place to break the journey and have a picnic and I particularly remember one such occasion which seemed to touch the highs and lows of family life all in the space of a few hours. The sun was beating down, the traffic was atrocious and very soon the car had become airless and stuffy – no air-condition back then - and the children, crammed up in the back, were exploring every known way to irritate each other. So when, eventually we reached our secret spot in a shady wood by a stream with cool water, shallow enough for paddling, the break was even more than usually welcome. Our picnic consisted of favourites, cold chicken, sausages, rolls and salad which we ate while the children cooled off in the water. Harmony was soon restored and my attention wandered to a pair of birds nearby. They, too, were enjoying the water, hopping in and out catching small insects and to judge by their comings and goings they had young to feed nearby. What were they, though? Wagtails certainly but lacking that sharp yellowness of yellow wagtails. Also they had blue-grey backs with flanks more lemon-coloured than yellow and tails noticeably longer than those of more familiar wagtails. I had never seen birds quite like these before but was pretty certain that they were grey wagtails, something that I confirmed later when I was able to unpack my bird-book.

Since then I have seen grey wagtails perhaps half-a-dozen times and each time memories of this first encounter and its idyllic surroundings come back sharp and clear. And so it was again when, earlier this summer, Lesley Jacklin told us that she had a pair nesting in a crevice in the back wall of her house in Lower Street. In the event this pair went on to raise two broods both from the same nest, feeding the young from insects caught from the small stream that flows along behind the houses on the east side of Lower Street, and in the process provided a summer of endless interest and delight for both Lesley and her visitors and neighbours. In some ways grey wagtails are an over-stated caricature of the wider family of wagtails, busier, more assertive and a good deal noisier than the others, their "chiz-it, chiz-it" calls not only betraying their presence but also providing a fair imitation of the tinkling of water running over pebbles along the steams where they spend so much of their lives. And then there are their tails, longer in relation to their bodies than those of other wagtails and always flicking up and down. If you want to photograph a grey wagtail, especially when near its young and emotions are running high, you need a shutter speed of at least a 500th of a second or you risk getting nothing more than a blur where the tail should be.

Like so many birds, once seen grey wagtails are fairly easy to recognise next time. The Sussex Bird Atlas describes them as fairly common passage migrants and winter visitors but scarce as residents, breeding only locally where there is a supply of fresh, clean, moving water. The Rother and the streams along the High Weald are county strongholds. Their cousins the yellow wagtails, on the other hand, are rarer with just a few breeding records in Sussex confined to Pevensey Levels and the grazed flood meadows around Rye Bay. They are, however spread widely across the Continent and on into the Gulf States where they have split themselves up into several different races each with its own distinctive markings. And just to complicate things further these races not only overlap geographically but also occasionally interbreed. And some stray across the Channel, thereby presenting endless challenges for our local twitchers.

The eminent ornithologist and wildlife painter Peter Scott tells an amusing story that illustrates the dilemma that these birds can create. The occasion was whilst having afternoon tea in the garden of the British Embassy in Jeddah and he found no less than 8 different races of wagtail strutting around on the lawn where he, his wife and hosts sat. Each bird exhibited its own distinctive variation in plumage, some with eye-stripes, some with varying amounts of blue on their heads, others with white-edged wing feathers and so on. Needless to say the great man made time to paint the birds and the resulting picture, reproduced in his book *Observations of Wildlife,* bears a footnote in which the artist apologises for having drawn the tails of the birds too long but excusing himself on the grounds that he had been so carried away by the elegance of the occasion and beauty of his subjects that he simply couldn't help himself.

Any notes on wagtails would be incomplete without a word about those with which we are most familiar, pied wagtails. And once again regional variations confuse things. First there is the nominate form which is called the white wagtail (*M a alba*) and is resident on the Continent and Scandinavia. The other is the pied wagtail (*M a yarrelli*) which is the one we see most often in this country. Occasionally the two forms stray into one another's territories and side by side it is possible to see that the white markings on *alba* are more dominant than on *yarrelli*. But seen in isolation it can be difficult to tell the one from the other.

September 2014

Life as a butterfly

Butterflies and flowering plants have existed side by side for over 150 million years and in that time their lives have become closely interlinked. Flowers provide butterflies with nectar and food for their caterpillars and repay them by distributing their pollen. But this mutual reliance carries risks just one example of which is that spring-hatching butterflies have evolved mouthparts designed to take nectar from spring-flowering plants and no other plants will do. So if, for any reason, the appearance of the two do not coincide, both suffer. And of course it is just such disturbance that is caused by changing climate. Butterflies require a year to complete their life-cycle, each species choosing in which stage to hibernate. This is a time for deep sleep and therefore carries the risk of predation and disease, but surprisingly not of extreme cold. In fact the opposite is the case; a mild winter brings the danger that the insect wakes up too soon and behaves as if it were spring before the food necessary to sustain revived activity is available.

Caterpillars are fussy eaters and female butterflies therefore take endless care to ensure that they lay their eggs on the right food plant. Some have developed sensors on the soles of their forelegs that enable them to check suitability by touch. Even so only about one in fifty survives to hatch into a caterpillar and even then the lucky ones face the risk that unseasonably dry weather will reduce what should have been a succulent and nutritious leaf to a frazzle. Others may suffer as did a colony of black hairstreaks on the North Downs that was wiped out by a farmer who unknowingly cut back the blackthorn bushes that sustained them just as their eggs were hatching. So now the only way to see this precious little woodland butterfly in this country is to visit a certain wood north of Oxford where, thanks to the diligence of conservationists, it still hangs on. Likewise their cousins, white-letter hairstreaks, whose larval food plant disappeared in the 1970s when beetles from Holland wiped out our elms. Other similar examples abound.

It is as caterpillars that all butterfly growth occurs. So caterpillars eat hugely and become plump juicy morsels for birds, specially those with young to feed. And those that escape birds face assaults from the hordes of solitary wasps whose charming ways include injecting eggs into their flesh, thereby ensuring fresh food for their hatching grubs. Caterpillars that survive these various vicissitudes turn into a hard-coated chrysalis that is usually suspended by a thin thread from a twig. Squash a chrysalis and all you'll find inside is a thick yellow fluid that will, in one of the wonders of nature, transform itself into an adult butterfly. This delicate process is easily upset by extremes in temperature that result in adults with aberrant colouration that were once the pride and joy of collectors.

It is as an adult butterfly that the mobility required for finding a mate, laying eggs and expanding distribution is possible. But before they can fly they need sun to raise their body temperatures to a minimum of 32°c. They also need the ultra-violet rays from sunlight to identify both their mates and the nectar-bearing flowers they feed from. In a nutshell, without sun butterflies cannot exist. The role of the male is to mate with as many females as possible, and of females to find the right place to lay eggs. Some species live several weeks and fly long distances and are often the most successful survivors. Others live just a few days and fly round in circles, never travelling more than 25 yards from their birthplace. Sometimes small groups become isolated so conservationists create corridors along which they can drift and form larger genetically more robust communities.

So with all this in mind let us see how butterflies have been getting on over the past three summers. 2012 was cold and sunless and as a result butterfly numbers across most species were at their lowest for 38 years. Autumn was little better although, surprisingly, a few that hibernate as adults appeared from nowhere and were still feeding up for the winter on late-flowering shrubs well into October. Winter was also exceptionally cold and so it continued throughout the spring and early summer of 2013. I remember writing here that I had seen almost none of those which hibernate as adults whose off-spring usually light up the countryside in mid-summer. And it was the same with all the other spring and early summer butterflies; woodland glades, chalk downs, gardens, everywhere – no butterflies to be seen anywhere.

Then in the last week of June the weather changed, the sun came out and stayed out until early September. And suddenly butterflies were everywhere; mid-summer species were, quite extraordinarily, mixed up with those that should have hatched a couple of months earlier and numbers everywhere were up. Nectar-bearing flowers for the adults and lush greenery for caterpillars were plentiful and flight periods were prolonged. And just to cap the happy scene there was a strong influx of migrants from the continent which included a couple of exciting rarities. One, the long-tailed blue was so tiny it could easily pass unnoticed, and the other, the much larger continental swallowtail which laid eggs and over-wintered here in West Sussex and up to 20 adults were seen flying around again this summer. So maybe we have a splendid new butterfly to add to our list of residents.

And so to 2014; the first 8 months are said to have been both the wettest and third warmest since records began and, wonderfully, butterflies have maintained the momentum of summer 2013. And even some rarities hitherto teetering on the verge of extinction and only found in seldom-visited places seem to have done well too. So based on these three years perhaps we can conclude that provided we humans refrain from tinkering with the places where they live, butterflies are well able to withstand the ups and downs of the recent erratic weather.

October 2014

Nature Matters

A new slant on a familiar story

"Everyone says something true about nature but while they may contribute little or nothing individually a great deal is amassed by bringing it all together".

So said Aristotle (384-322BC), a man often called the father of science. Now, some 2,350 years on, modern technology has enabled David Christian, a historian working at Macquarie University in Sydney, to assemble a history of our universe that starts with its creation some 13.7 billion years ago. This story has been told many times before but usually in separate bits; cosmologists dealing with the origin and nature of the universe, biologists with the growth and spread of life, anthropologists with human institutions and beliefs, and so on. But Christian's achievement is to bring all these threads of knowledge together and tell the story as one composite whole.

It helps us to grasp the scale of this project by chopping those 13.7 billion years into more digestible bites. So let us progress immediately to the point at which life on Earth appeared for the first time. New fossils continue to be found but a working date for this might be 3600 million years ago. If we then re-scale all subsequent time as if it were one calendar year we can regard each day as if it were 10 million years. On this basis by mid-November life had evolved no further than tiny worms that burrowed through the mud. One week later fish appeared and by mid-December little lizards scuttled across the beach to become dinosaurs and birds. Then late in the afternoon on New Year's Eve a species of primate came out from the forests onto the plains and stood up on their hind-legs the better to see across the open spaces. After a while they began to till the land and grow food. They refined their speech, decorated caves with paintings and established patterns of behaviour and culture that lie at the heart of today's civilizations. By mid-night they had accomplished all that we see about us today.

So well done us humans!! But Christian's story must also acknowledge that every other life-form in existence today has an evolutionary path that reaches back in time as far as our own and, even if on a smaller scale, has been just as successful. Had that not been so they would not have survived. True, we have developed abilities which make us dominant but this is often because we have built tools to do things that others do unaided. One example is a swallow that commutes each year between here and South Africa, returning each spring to precisely the same nest. Such a feat is well beyond us, so we build an airplane with a sophisticated navigation system and do it that way.

David Christian calls his project The Big History and since so much of his material comes from the sciences one may wonder why the compilation has been undertaken by a historian. He has been working on the project for 20 years and has been careful to gain peer approval along the way. In fact he tells us that when he presented his project to an assembly of scientists in California and invited comments only one, a noted cosmologist, raised a small caveat concerning the amount of energy released at the dawn of time. It may have crossed Christian's mind that such trivia is as nothing compared with Aristotle's firm belief that the redstarts he saw in the summer transformed themselves into the robins he saw in the winter.

Six years ago the recently retired founder of Microsoft, Bill Gates, came across Christian's work presented in a series of easily digestible instalments on the internet and liked what he saw so much that he immediately gave him $10 million to promote his work within the field of education. Now it is used intermittently in America, Australia, Scotland, Holland and Korea and is widely read on the internet; Bill Gates is quoted as saying that he only wishes that it had been available when he was at school. Whether or not this format is, indeed, right for the class-room is for others to decide but whatever the answer, it must be the case that the underlying scientific research is best left to the appropriate academic faculties. But that does not alter the fact that Christian's story provides a fresh stimulus for an enquiring mind and is a timely reminder of where our present-day world stands in the context of the history of the universe.

So finally, let us take a glimpse at the wildlife on our own doorstep and see how it is coping with ever-changing conditions. These notes often mention the shifts in distribution of birds and insects brought about by the warming of our climate and there are two new and recent examples; black-backed stilts and golden orioles have both crossed the Channel for the first time this spring and nested in this country, thereby becoming only the latest of a steady stream of exotic new-comers that have not in the past come this far north. And then there is the case of the family of chiffchaffs that have been using our garden as a play-ground since late September and on into October. In normal times we might have expected such a party to be on the verge of pushing off back to Spain or beyond. Chiffchaffs arrive here in early April and the males announce themselves by singing their famous *chiff chaff chaff chiff* song. They keep this up until the end of June, time enough to fit in one if not two broods. But our family looks of an age to suggest that the warm September prompted their parents to raise a late third brood. This in itself is unusual and if they then stay here all winter (they are still here into the second week in October) they will be swelling the numbers of summer visitors that now find our winters sufficiently benign to risk staying on here all year.

November 2014

Nature Matters

A look at the year that was

As in life so, too, in nature - one thing inevitably leads to another. This time last year we were on the verge of a prolonged period of gales, heavy rain and floods but, surprisingly, temperatures that were well above average. These conditions persisted into spring and the consequences for wildlife were various. Ground-nesting birds, particularly those which nest close to ponds and rivers, were flooded out. Flooding also took its toll amongst small terrestrial mammals and this in turn put pressure on the predators which rely on them for food. And so it goes on. Assessing the full extent of the damage will take time but already the experts say that barn owls, as just one example, have this year declined by 91%.

However it was not all bad. In conditions that were both wet and warm the obvious winners were plants and shrubs so that spring blossom and wild flowers did well. And to cap it all bees and other pollinators also found things to their liking, something confirmed in last month's magazine where Kathy Haigh told us about her experiences as a bee-keeper. Thus the scene was set for an autumn where the hedgerows were laden with fruit. Elderberry, blackberry and hip roses all lit up the countryside and makers of home-made sloe gin did not have far to go to find a good supply of nice juicy fruit. At which point perhaps I should confess to a personal prejudice. I always prefer to make sloe gin by marinating the sloes in vodka rather than gin, the latter having already been flavoured with juniper, coriander and other exotic botanicals in accordance with secret recipes known only to the most trusted of the trade's elders. Gordons, the patriarchs in the art of gin-making, sometimes produce a limited quantity of sloe gin just for a bit of fun, using only highly rectified neutral alcohol similar to vodka as a base, and if you can find a bottle I recommend it; it is almost as good as ours.

But back to the matter in hand; this richly fertile spring resulted in an autumn which has provided plenty of winter food for wildlife in general and birds in particular. The first birds to arrive were as usual the Scandinavian thrushes; redwings and fieldfares. They flood in off the North Sea arriving on the east coast any time around mid-September and spread across the country feeding on berries as they go. When they've finished these they go onto open land to forage for insects and, if the ground is frozen, as a last resort they come to bird tables and frighten away all our gently-nurtured little garden birds. Other arrivals from Scandinavia are bramblings, members of the finch family which remain in flocks and make for beech woods to eat the fallen mast. They are a bit like chaffinches but more colourful and easily identified by their white rumps.

Another group of winter visitors that can easily pass unnoticed are foreign versions of our own residents. Amongst the most prominent are wood pigeons, the visitors remaining in flocks of several hundred, wheeling round searching for places to eat. Our resident wood pigeons, by contrast, are either solitary or form only small groups and are better mannered. In addition to the arrival of visitors, there is a great amount of seasonal movement amongst our native birds and one that seems to be increasing in our area is the raven. We have twice recently seen a couple whilst walking late in the day on Lords Piece. In fact the second time we witnessed a strange happening; one of the ravens must have strayed into the local sparrowhawk's territory causing the latter to fly up and give chase. The disparity in size was laughable and the larger raven may not even have noticed the frantically dive-bombing hawk. The "chase" continued for about 200 yards before the hawk ducked into a tree, no doubt satisfied that he had demonstrated the requisite degree of machismo. I related this story to a friend who knows a bit about birds of prey and it seems that when it comes to hot-headed but futile chases sparrowhawks have form; he tells me that he once saw one foolhardy enough to attack a red kite. But all this aside, my favourite experience this autumn was reserved until just before filing these notes when we awoke to find 6 Cattle Egrets foraging for insects amongst the cattle just below our bedroom window - yet one more example of the way in which our native fauna is being augmented by newly arrived exotica from far to the south.

And now a story from the heart of our village. It was the last Sunday in October and we were just leaving Church after morning service. A group of children, also part of our congregation, were gathered on the path outside examining a small butterfly asleep on the tip of a grass stem which one of them was holding. I was called in to assist with identification and the insect was transferred onto the palm of my hand where, to the delight of the children, the warmth was sufficient to cause it to open its wings and reveal the beautiful lilac blue fringed in white of a male Common Blue. What's more it was in perfect condition, suggesting that it was newly hatched. But here's the thing; Common Blues are not like some of the larger butterflies which fly long into autumn, braving the weather and then hibernating as adults. Common Blues have two broods each year, the second of which produces caterpillars that go into hibernation any time between late June and September and that's the last we see of adult Common Blues until next year's hatch. So where had this little butterfly that so thrilled the children come from? My guess is that as a baby caterpillar of the second generation it had gone into hibernation in August when it was very cold expecting to sleep through until next spring. But September was exceptionally warm so the sleeping caterpillar had woken up. Perhaps thinking it was already spring he had munched his way through the trefoils which grow in the churchyard and when fully grown had pupated. But the weather remained warm, so mistaking things for next May he hatched into a butterfly. But it wasn't - it was only 26th October.

December 2014.

Nature Matters

Our countryside & its wildlife

As a new year dawns, so the village settles to the task of preparing a new Neighbourhood Development Plan that will tell the planning authorities the type of place we wish to live in over the next 20 years. So this seems a good time to remind ourselves of the wider countryside that surrounds Fittleworth and contributes so much to the character of our village. The immediate features are obvious; the Downs, the River Rother and surrounding valley to the south, the woodlands to the north and the belt of greensand upon which sit the near-by Commons to east and west. But interspersed with this there is much else. As typical examples there are four reserves nearby, each managed by the Sussex Wildlife Trust (SWT) and each typical of different facets of our local countryside.

Two, The Mens and Ebernoe Common, are predominantly woodland. Both reserves offer a good range of woodland fauna and flora and each has its own specialities; montjak deer on The Mens, and 14 of the 16 bat species native to this country on Ebernoe. However a more significant difference between the two can be traced back to human activities 6 centuries ago when The Mens was a centre of glass-making and the furnaces were fuelled by charcoal obtained from the local beech woods. This suited local Commoners who owned the coppicing rights and relied on the sale of the wood for a livelihood. Subsequently when The Mens was threatened by the widespread Wealden forest clearance the Commoners invoked their rights and The Mens was spared. Thus when glass-making ceased the ancient woodland was still standing and remains so until acquired by SWT. Since then the only work undertaken is that needed to ensure public safety. Thus the natural processes of growth, decay and regeneration still proceed unhindered.

By contrast Ebernoe Common still provides evidence of the production of iron which was prevalent across the Weald in the 1500s and Furnace Pond, constructed to power the iron furnace, today provides the reserve with one of its most prominent habitats for wildlife. Another industry from times past, evidence of which survives on Ebernoe, is the manufacture of bricks. Dating back to the 1700s and using locally dug clay (samples of which still cling relentlessly to the boots of visitors on a wet day) the business carried on into 1930s and both the kiln and moulding shed, now restored, are scheduled as ancient monuments.

Two other reserves nearby, Iping/Stedham Commons just west of Midhurst and Lavington Common south of Petworth, are fine examples of lowland heath. At first glance these landscapes can look barren and forbidding and indeed when he saw Ashdown in 1882, whilst touring south-east England on his horse, William Cobbett later described it as "verily the most villainously ugly spot I ever saw in England". To anyone who has visited our local heathlands when the heather is in bloom, this will seem a harsh judgement.

Lowland heaths were, for centuries, used for the grazing of farm animals. Bracken was cut for winter bedding and gorse was used for fuel and animal food and this made for a unique and rare landscape. However a century ago these activities ceased, leaving birch, bracken and coarse grasses free to grow unchecked. Some of the land has since been converted into improved farmland, some taken for housing and some left as scrub. Today only about 10% survives as the typical lowland heathlands that are unique to the acidic low-nutrient sand belts of southern England.

Restoring and maintaining these places takes time and often involves the use of heavy machinery in conjunction with controlled grazing by cattle with fences and gates and this provokes public outcry. But few will dispute that the results bring rewards, both scenically and in wealth of wildlife. People visit these places to see the extraordinary relationship between ants and silver-studded blue butterflies, the ants defending the butterfly throughout its life from predators, knowing that their caterpillars, when massaged, exude nutritious fluids for them to lick. Others come in the late evening to see and hear nightjars and others to find rare bog asphodel and insectivorous sundew plants growing in the acid bogs - both of which, incidentally, also grow in the bog at the bottom end of Hesworth Common.

Much other excellent work is being done to safeguard the beauty of the Sussex countryside and its wildlife and these notes can only scratch the surface. Never-the-less wise words come back to me spoken by a naturalist I met once in Lithuania. I had remarked to him on the beauty of his countryside and the richness of its wildlife and he had replied that his worry about Britain was that similar places may soon be confined to a series of theme parks. An exaggeration perhaps, but a warning none-the-less. So remembering this, it is good to hear that the focus amongst conservationists is now switching to landscape-scale planning. This concept is designed to address situations all too common today where individual species become isolated, habitats are exhausted, the gene-bank weakens and the colony dies out. At present conservationists make corridors between habitats along which threatened species can wander naturally. This works well with things like weak-flying butterflies, but is both limited in scope and labour-intensive. Landscape planning takes countryside conservation onto a higher level but requires widespread consensus. So it is excellent to hear that the individual County Wildlife Trusts across all of south-east England have come together to create integrated plans designed to protect the countryside and its wildlife.

Their stated vision is;

A countryside which is as rich in wildlife as it was in yesteryear but helps to maintain our climate, produces our food and replenishes our spirits – a countryside for the 21st century.

January 2015

Winter musings

There is a certain stillness and beauty about woodlands in winter. These are times when the trees are bare of leaves and the tracery of the branches stands out clear against a cold blue sky. It is also a good time to see birds, with the added advantage that so many of the summer-visiting little brown jobs that confusingly all look the same have not yet arrived. Woods are not the only places that take on extra beauty in winter and the presence of a little wildlife always adds interest. The way in which these two elements complement one another was evident recently when a selection of the year's best nature photographs appeared in a Sunday colour supplement. The photographs, all of animals, were so tightly cropped that all meaning was lost and as a result the pictures were, frankly, boring. Shortly afterwards I happened to spot a blackbird sitting in amongst the branches of an ash tree just outside our back door. The bird was silhouetted against a sky tinged with pink and the scene was redolent of cold winter and encroaching twilight. This bird was, clearly about to face a major hazard, surviving a long, cold winter night. A photo of this every-day scene would have conveyed all this and far exceeded in interest the posed portraits in the magazine.

The Japanese are a people in whose culture there is a deeply embedded desire to find places of profound simplicity, free of distractions to which they can retire to contemplate in peace the beauty of nature. Their name for this is *yukimi*. Brought to Japan from China in the 16th century by Zen Buddhist monks, *yukimi* often reaches a peak at certain times of year – winter for snow-scenes, spring for almond blossom and autumn for the colours of maple leaves – and is best viewed from certain vantage points. Sometimes there are tea-houses where monks prepare tea in a ceremony called *yukimi chakai*. There is a delicate sanctity about these occasions that is echoed in many forms of Japanese art.

Another manifestation of *yukimi* is found in the classic Japanese Stone Gardens. These are man-made spaces often no larger than a tennis court. Each is designed to reflect an aspect of nature in its simplest form. This then acts as a catalyst for contemplation, a bench being placed at the optimum viewing spot. Simplicity helps to focus attention and the ultimate in minimalist design is no more than a stretch of sand carefully raked to suggest the ripples on the surface of water. Visitors from the west are often bewildered by such places and cynics may think they are witnessing some form of orchestrated daydreaming. But in truth we here are probably tapping into much the same restorative pleasures when we sit quietly watching birds coming and going around our feeders.

I once visited the Atomic Bomb Museum in Nagasaki which stands at the epicentre of the bomb that exploded there on 9th August 1945. It depicts in relentless detail the horror of that event and I cannot remember ever being so moved. But another thing sticks in my mind; we had stopped in front of the main exhibit which showed in horrifying detail life-sized models of people, some carrying their babies, rushing from their burning homes, skin melting from their bodies as if it were molten wax flowing down the side of a candle. Visitors were visibly near to tears: all except a party of Japanese schoolchildren who stood pointing and laughing as if watching something at a zoo. My concern was simply that if these children had been judged old enough to visit the museum, surely its awful but important message should have been explained to them beforehand. It all seemed so out of character. Those same children will now be approaching their 50th birthdays. Thus the preservation of the wonderful and unique cultural traditions for which the Japanese are so well-known is now in their hands.

Now in a different sphere, word comes from Caerlaverock in Dumfriesshire that amongst the 30,000 barnacle geese that come down from Svalbard each winter is one bird that is a record 28 years old and has therefore clocked up 120,000 miles making the bi-annual flight. This news reminds me that when we set up a feeding station for a family of robins to entertain visitors to last year's Garden Trail the most frequent question I had was how long do robins live. Knowing how vulnerable small birds are to predators with few living out their full life-spans, I took a punt and said from 2 to 4 years, depending on the neighbourhood cats. Later I re-read David Lack's book on robins and learned the truth. When kept out of harms way in captivity the average life-span is 10 years during which time a pair will lay on average ten eggs per year. This means that if all their progeny also survive the pair will have notched up a life-total of 100 children and an astonishing 20 million grandchildren. Getting to their funeral would be like fighting your way through a swarm of migrating locusts.

But of course life in the wild is packed with hazards and the rate of mortality is massive. As with all animals a stable population comes about when there is an equilibrium between births and deaths and the first thing we learn about robins is that 77% die during their first winter when their naivety puts them at greatest risk. Put another way, this means that about ¾ of each year's hatch never live long enough even to breed once. This sounds catastrophic but it is not because arithmetic tells us that, to maintain a stable population, the remaining 23% only require to live on average only 15 months. And this astonishingly low figure is confirmed by the numbers of ringed corpses recovered. Sad to think of all those robins killed by predators or otherwise failing to survive the rigours of life but that's the way nature works. And there is a consolation. As with any average there are highs and lows; some canny robins have been known to survive in the wild to the ripe old age of 11. So the robin that comes and sits beside you when you're gardening could, after all, still be the same old friend from previous years.

February 2015

Nature Matters

Three birds & a dog called Fred

One of my favourite boyhood books was by Eric Hosking. It had photographs of birds taken with a camera that required all settings to be made manually and therefore many were taken at the nest from a hide, thus enabling both exposure and focus to be pre-set. Although most of his work pre-dates colour photography no-one has surpassed Hosking in the art of capturing the essential ethos of his subjects and because much of his work was done in the fenlands of East Anglia there must be many birders who were first attracted to these very special places by the magic of his photographs. One of his favourite subjects inseparable in my mind from the fenland reed-beds are bitterns. Members of the heron family but smaller than grey herons they are best known for the massive booming sound made by males during the breeding season. Another particular feature is their superb camouflage which enables them to stand still with head stretched upward and blend seamlessly into the background of a reed-bed. If a wind disturbs the reeds bitterns even sway in unison. This enables them to escape the attention of their enemies and remain invisible to the prey-fish which they feed on.

Hoskings's photographs of bitterns had persuaded me that in this country they were confined to the reed-beds of East Anglia and I was fired with a determination to go and see them. However my first encounter, some sixty years ago, was in a very different place not far from here. I was wandering around the fields just to the south of Chingford Pond in Burton Park with a good friend Mike. It was early in January and there had been a fresh fall of snow. We were on private land but had the farmer's permission to shoot any pheasants we put up. Mike had brought along Fred, a dachshund who was as good as a spaniel at working the thickets but, true to his breed, less obedient. Fred was well-known around the local pubs where owners kept a bowl large enough for a quarter-pint of draft Guinness. This was for Fred and would be downed in a one-er. But because his internal plumbing had perforce undergone some modifications he was quickly obliged to excuse himself outside. Just the one was enough for Fred and when all was done he would sit quietly beside Mike until it was time to go home.

So back to bitterns. We were crossing the field behind the lake when Fred decided to work the nearby reed-bed and it was not long before he put up this unusual but to me instantly recognisable large brown bird. At the same instant I saw out of the corner of my eye Mike raising his gun in the belief, no doubt, that he was onto a hen pheasant. Mike was a good shot but had lost a leg in the war and on rough ground in snow he needed a crutch, so was slower to raise his gun than might otherwise have been the case. This gave me time to shout a warning not to shoot and mercifully he didn't. Even in those days when public attitudes were nothing like they are today shooting a bittern would not have been a good idea. Today when the countryside is constantly scrutinised by armies of knowledgeable naturalists we know much more about things; these birds, we now know, spread across southern England in winter and most years one or two come onto the lakes at Burton Park. But because of their secretive nature and excellent camouflage they are seldom seen. Indeed the occasional sighting always causes excitement, even in their breeding grounds in Norfolk, a fact that has been turned to their advantage by the staff at the RSPB reserve at Titchwell; if you see a bittern there and tell the wardens the occasion is marked by a little ceremony and a badge is pinned onto your lapel. What's more there will be additional badges for anyone else near-by who, caught up in the general merriment, also claims to have seen the bird. Only after they are all securely fastened to the lapels of each claimant will you be told that "by the way, there is a charge of £1 per badge."

We usually think of chiffchaffs as one of several warbler species that come here in the spring, sing sweetly, raise a family and in the autumn return to Africa. But less often seen is another race of chiffchaff, *P.c. tristis*, from Siberia that pass through briefly on passage. Expert birders can tell one race from the other and until recently the schedules of the two meant that if they met at all it was only in passing. However with our warmer winters habits are changing and individuals from both races are content to make this their home for the winter. The inevitable consequence is that the two races are meeting, and creating new hybrids. Evidence that this is already happening comes from a flock composed of both races that have spent the winter around the Coldwaltham water-treatment plant amongst which are individuals with unmistakable signs of mixed-race plumage.

By way of contrast one of the most sedentary of all our birds are ravens. Until the early 19th century they were abundant across the whole country breeding in both woodlands and cliffs, but persecution mostly by gamekeepers brought them to the verge of extinction. Nesting in Sussex ceased in 1880 and only started again in 2001. Since then numbers have increased each year helped by nest-building that has spread from cliffs where they were vulnerable to predation into woodland which provide better protection. Evidence that numbers are building up comes from the establishment of a night-time roost of about 40 birds up on the Downs. Ravens can be distinguished from crows and rooks by their heavier appearance, stout beaks and, in flight, by slightly wedge-shaped tails and pointed wings. They also have a distinct call best written as "pruk pruk". Ravens are clumsy on the ground but accomplished flyers, sometimes suddenly turning belly upwards and gliding thus for short distances; or nose-diving with wings closed. Such frivolities are a surprise coming from a bird of such stolid, not to say boring, appearance.

May 2015

Birds in spring

Every spring approximately 600 different species of birds raise families in the British Isles. Of these 51 are migrants and will depart again when our summer is over. By catching and ringing these migrants a bank of knowledge has been built up so that we now know where they come from and the routes they take. We also know the different often complicated ways they navigate. The simplest are those that use their eyes to follow familiar landmarks. But others travel by night using stars. Some use the sun and can compensate for its movement across the sky. And a few have sensors in their brains that enable them to navigate by using the Earth's magnetic field. Long flights put pressure on supplies of energy and many large birds use thermal currents for gliding. Indeed flocks of cranes coming up from Africa to their breeding grounds in Eastern Europe use the warm spring air rising above cities for bouncy, providing dwellers below with an eagerly awaited visual treat. Smaller birds fly with fast-flapping wings and use up energy quickly. They feed up before setting out but even so, fly overland where possible, knowing that food-stops are needed along the way. And then there are penguins; they waddle unsteadily over many miles of ice and are much loved by wildlife film-makers anxious to inject a touch of comedy into their programmes.

It used to be said that the impulse to migrate was triggered by changes in the length of daylight. Support for this view came from experiments wherein birds were subjected in autumn to artificial daylight that increased to suggest spring. This induced the birds to fly north instead of south. But the impact of recent global warming suggests other factors are at play. Maybe they simply follow the food; when the midges hatch (or don't) its time to move. After all the main concern of any bird is its safety and availability of food and once families are raised they are free to move where they wish.

But one question remains; why do so many birds travel so far when what they seek can also be had much nearer to hand? For example arctic terns famously migrate backwards and forwards between the Arctic and the Antarctic, a round journey of 36,000 kilometres. The rewards cannot possibly justify such risky and energy-sapping journeys. Furthermore how did the birds first get to know what awaits them 18,000 kilometres away? As ever, David Attenborough has the answer; when the planet was in the grip of the ice age ancestral arctic terns lived within the inter-glacial areas of Africa and could feed year-round without moving. But when the ice-age was coming to an end 11,000 years ago the glaciers began to recede back towards the poles, exposing new food-rich land. The terns followed the food and, with the passing of time, set up a migration northward in the northern hemisphere summer and southward in the southern hemisphere summer, leading eventually to the incredible journeys of today.

Once birds have settled into their nesting quarters there is much to be done. The process is the same for both locals and migrants; males squabble over territories and, this settled, start to call. Calls come in many forms; melodious song, quacks, squawks and hoots are just a few. But all have three purposes. The first is to proclaim his species. Second is a warning to rivals to keep off his patch, and finally he is inviting females to join him. This done there follows a ritual of courtship which varies from species to species but usually includes a display of manliness that demonstrates his suitability for fatherhood. Once a relationship is secured the pair move on to the usual parental duties, the sharing of which varies with species. With some both parents build the nest and take turns with incubation; in others these are attended to by the female, leaving the male to hunt for food. In the extreme case of phalaropes the female does no more than lay eggs. This done she joins the other local ladies and collectively they keep their toiling spouses within sight but take no part in any of the everyday family chores.

Finally the vexed question of fidelity. Some birds mate for life and spend all year in each other's company. Within this group there is a token courtship each spring as the breeding season approaches but it amounts to little more than an act of re-affirmation. Others, such as puffins, go their separate ways after nesting but meet again the following spring at the previous year's nest-site. They greet each other with a shaking of beaks and an affectionate little dance and should one of a pair fail to show the survivor sits forlornly by the nest and is unlikely to re-mate that season. Sometimes unmated birds seek solace with another of the same sex, the two sitting side by side contentedly watching the hurly-burly of life around them. Gannets are an extreme example; a nesting colony of gannets is so tightly packed that incubating birds can reach across to a neighbour to steal food without even standing up. Squabbles within this community are thus never-ending and unmated males have been quick to establish an area to one side where they can pass their time in peace and quiet. Birders call this area The Club and it can easily be seen from a distance because members of the club lack the chestnut-tinged head of a breeding male gannet. Thus the general impression is of a purer whiteness.

Other birds typified by tits bond afresh each year in trysts more often honoured in the breach than not. Indeed researchers have found that promiscuity within these birds is such that the paternity of any single clutch of eggs may be shared between up to three local males. Nor can the hen be sure that she alone has laid all the eggs she is sitting on; it may be that a neighbour had popped in when she was off the nest and added one of her own. Never-the-less there is always one male on hand who comes to the fore when necessary to share in the general duties of parenthood, and no matter what we think about these shenanigans, they undoubtedly satisfy the Darwinian requirements for survival.

April 2015

From anther to ovule; the pollinators

With the advance of spring insects that have been dormant all winter start to flit amongst the flower-heads and in doing so they spread pollen. As a measure of how important this simple act is Albert Einstein has told us that, without it, we humans would run out of food within four years. Pollination is the process whereby the male pollen produced by a flower's anther is transferred to the female ovule, thus triggering the development of fertile seeds. But because self-pollination weakens the strain a way for distributing pollen is required, and this is where insects come in; flowers produce nectar to attract insects and when they come to feed they get dusted with pollen. The insect then transports the pollen to the next flower it visits where it rubs off on the ovule, and the job is done.

Usually the first on the scene each year are the queen bumblebees and I have seen them as early as January flying over a couple of inches of snow. Normally though they come out of hibernation around April or May when they can often be seen walking around on the ground searching for a good place to establish a nest. Once found they settle down to lay the eggs that were fertilised the previous autumn. These eggs then hatch into larvae which in turn become the worker-bees whose duty it is to forage for nectar and tend to the colony. These worker bees are non-breeding females, the organs which would otherwise be used for laying eggs (ovipositors) having evolved into the kit with which they sting. The queen continues to lay eggs throughout the summer, the later ones developing into the next generation of queens and males which immediately leave the nest, disperse and mate with those from other colonies. The males then die, their mission complete, and the females with their bodies full of fertile eggs go into hibernation until the following spring when they wake up as the new generation of queens.

Honey bees are related to bumblebees but differ by producing honey and wax, thereby establishing a long and close affinity with us humans. The oldest known honey bee has been entombed within a drop of amber for 80 million years and 8,000-year-old cave paintings in Valencia depict hunters taking honey from a wild bee's nest. Worker bees forage over a range of 3 miles on wings that beat 200 times per second. They visit up to 10,000 flower heads a day and when finished they return to precisely the same spot within their nest from which they departed. They then perform a little dance that tells other workers exactly where to go next day to find the best nectar-rich flowers. After about five weeks of assiduous toil a honeybee dies from exhaustion, happy in the knowledge that its lifetime achievement has been to produce just a quarter of an ounce of honey.

The wider family of bees, the order hymenoptera, also includes ants, wasps, and sawflies amounting in total to 6,200 different species, just in Britain. They all play a part in pollination but so do mice, bats, beetles and wind. So let us confine ourselves to those that also add beauty to our summer scene and move on to the infinitely more attractive hover flies. These little gems are all-too-often overlooked by both naturalists and yet there is seldom a flowerbed or bank of wild flowers which is without them. There are over 230 species in this country and few even have common names. They are true flies, typified by just one pair of wings, something which separates them from wasps and bees which some try to mimic in the belief that their attackers will be deterred by the thought of getting stung. Hover flies feed by hovering with fast wing-beats and dipping their antennae into the flower to drink nectar. They also perform a second service for gardeners by laying their eggs in places where their larva can feed on aphids.

Hover fly mimics a wasp

Butterflies and moths are also important pollinators which provide examples of where the relationship between flower and insect has become so specialised that it is limited to just a few species. Thus some flowers have developed shapes that require the associated butterflies to have mouth-parts specially adapted to reach the nectar. Other flowers produce smells that mimic the pheromones which are used by night-flying moths to find mates. Colours are also important and of course there are the orchids, mostly of the bee family, that have lips that mimic with extraordinary accuracy the abdomen of a female bee, the strategy being to entice a male to mate with it and in the process cover himself with pollen.

Bee orchid

This interaction between insects and flowers has evolved over millions of years and is carefully balanced. As a result if one suffers adversity so does the other. So perhaps we should not be surprised that the massive changes that have occurred in our countryside during the past half century have put the relationship under immense pressure. Just two examples make the point, both taken from the 70% of Britain that is farmed. The first is that changes in land management has resulted in the loss of 95% of our flower-rich grassland. On top of this new pesticides have been widely used, often before their full impact was properly assessed, and the result has been the unintended loss of many beneficial species. Clearly these are matters for the experts but, remembering those words of Einstein, it does seem that in the head-long battle to increase productivity their weapon of choice has often been the boomerang.

May 2015.

PS; last month when extolling the elegance of flying cranes the word "bouncy" appeared where "buoyancy" was intended. My apologies to readers, our Editor and also to cranes.

A cuckoo's secrets

Until the advent of the internet nowhere was the competition to hear the first cuckoo of the year more fierce than in the letters pages of *The Times* and two which illustrate the potential hazards of an over-hasty claim are both from a B. Lydekker FRS. In the first, dated 6th February 1913, he tells readers excitedly that he had just heard the "unmistakable full double-call of a cuckoo; of that there can be not the slightest doubt". Then six days later he writes again to apologise, saying that he was deceived in his report by a local bricklayer's mate who he has interviewed and who admits that his imitations are so good that he can call up another cuckoo "without the aid of any instrument". For further enlightenment upon the question of imitation we must wait several years for The Reverend K. H. MacDermott to write to say that the perfect rendition of a male cuckoo is achieved on the piano by playing the notes D and B flat, as immortalized by Beethoven in the second movement of his Pastoral Symphony. As this work was composed long after Beethoven had become deaf and was therefore relying on his memory cuckoos must have retained their exact pitch for nearly 200 years.

Another matter, this one keeping the great ones bickering amongst themselves for years, was how a bird as large as a cuckoo could lay its egg in a nest as small as those of its chosen hosts. Two theories held sway, the first that the cuckoo laid its egg some distance from the host nest, swallowed it and then flew in to regurgitate it direct into the nest. And the second, that she squatted on the rim of the host nest and using muscles unique to such birds was able to squirt the egg in without sitting. Each view was fiercely championed by an eminent egg-collector. (This was in the 1920s when egg collecting, or oology, was acceptable) Leading for the regurgitaters was The Reverend F.C.R. Jourdain, known to friend and foe alike as the pugnacious prelate and a man not inclined to spend much time listening to the views of others. The squirters' case was championed by Percy Bunyard, a fruit grower who was almost stone deaf. When debating this matter, therefore, Bunyard was able to discomfort his short-tempered adversary by waving a long-handled hearing trumpet in front of his face, the better to catch the flow of his fierce argument. As a result meetings of the British Ornithological Club where this faintly laughable issue was debated over several years drew large numbers who came as much for the jolly sense of theatre as for the substance of the matter.

Time passed without agreement so a working party was set up and after 7 years of fieldwork it was decided with the aid of photographs that the squirters were correct. And what's more these researches unearthed much new knowledge about cuckoos. For instance they discovered that cuckoos spend hours hidden under cover surreptitiously reviewing the scene in order not to arouse the suspicion of small birds. When ultimately a target nest has been identified the cuckoo darts in briefly, lays its egg and is gone in a matter of seconds. The visit is timed to coincide with the laying of the foster-mother's first egg which they remove when laying their own. In all these furtive activities the cuckoo is aided by its resemblance to the dreaded sparrow hawk

The colours of cuckoo eggs are variable within a range of shades of brown background with darker brown speckles the purpose being to ensure that they resemble the colour of foster-bird eggs sufficiently to pass unnoticed. As they become more experienced cuckoos learn to choose foster-parents whose eggs most closely resemble their own. But therein lies the danger that this helps a target bird to learn how to identify an alien egg and reject it. Three such birds are chaffinches, reed buntings and blackcaps all of which were once parasitized but now escape attention, presumably because those cuckoos which used them have failed to breed and so died out. We know that cuckoo numbers are down and this may part of the reason.

Eggs are laid every two days, each bird laying about 12 a season. Cuckoos seldom lay more than one egg per nest so that the newly-hatched baby cuckoo will find itself in company with several host-eggs and/or nestlings. These it simply tips out of the nest using a shallow dip in the small of its back to hold the load steady during the lifting and tipping process. This done, the impostor has the undivided attention of its foster-parents and soon grows to be around eight times their weight. But there is more to parenting than just stuffing food into ever-open mouths; chicks learn the calls of their species by close association with their parents and this imprinting occurs during the first four days of their lives. Yet during this short period the baby cuckoo must surely take the chat of its foster-parents as the model. Whilst this may help it in due course to identify suitable foster-parents for its own young, it does not teach males the famed "cuckoo" call of Beethoven's music, or females their much softer bubbling sounds. And a cuckoo flying around sounding like, say, a reed warbler would not easily find a mate. The best explanation on offer is that from the general cacophony of bird-calls reaching it from the surrounding countryside the baby cuckoo is able to pick out those produced either by its genetic parents or other adult cuckoos - none of which it has ever seen - recognise them and when grown up reproduce them with unfailing accuracy. If true, this is extraordinary!

June 2015

The Red Kite's story

Early in the spring of 1990 a small team of naturalists and film-makers gathered at the RSPB reserve at Dinas. just north of Llanovery in Wales. Their purpose was to reconnoitre the surrounding countryside in preparation for the shooting of a film called *Kite Country*. It was to be one episode in a six-part series for Channel 4 under the overall title *Birdscape*. The project was the idea of Bruce Pearson, a wild-life artist well-known for his ability to bring together through his paintings the beauty of both his subjects and the places they inhabit.

1990 was a crucial time in the roller-coaster history of red kites in this country. After decades of persecution they were just beginning to re-establish themselves, in this, their former stronghold in Wales. Egg-collectors were still a huge problem, sixteen nests having been robbed in the previous two years and it seemed that the illegal market was so strong that even a penalty for those convicted of £2,000 per egg was no deterrent. But the tide was turning and by the end of 1990 there were estimated to be up to 70 young on the wing making a total of about 250 red kites living in this, their last remaining redoubt in the British Isles.

All this makes it hard to believe that seven centuries ago red kites were our commonest birds of prey and would have been seen in great numbers wheeling and circling over recently-cleared woodlands searching for earthworms and carrion, much as rooks, crows and jackdaws do today. Indeed the close proximity of these birds to human life led William Turner to write to the Swiss naturalist Gesner that "We have kites in England the like of which I have seen nowhere else. Our birds dare to snatch bread from children and fish from women and handkerchiefs off hedges when building their nests." Even if this was a bit of an exaggeration one thing we know for certain is that their predilection to scavenge meant that red kites performed a civic duty as garbage collectors, removing from the streets litter that was both foul-smelling and a source of disease. Indeed, for this service they were, for a while at least, accorded the benefits of royal protection.

But this was a high-point in their fortunes. As public sanitation improved red kites lost their royal protection and, whilst still tolerated in towns, the Vermin Acts of 1532 and 1566 put a price on their heads in the countryside and there is plenty of evidence to show the scale of the slaughter inflicted by bounty-hunters. It seems that even Churchwardens had cottoned onto the potential for income, the accounts of many rural churches showing that at one penny a bird a significant incremental income could be earned. But the real killer for red kites, as for so many birds of prey, was the Game Act of 1831 and the perfection of the double-barrelled shotgun. These in combination relentlessly drove red kites to a point where, by 1900, their last refuge in Britain was the remote valleys of Wales. This, of course, only served to increase the value of their eggs and when in 1905 The British Ornithology Club, fore-runners to the RSPB, achieved the enactment of legislation that permitted protection of nests the move failed because egg collectors were making so much money that they simply bribed the hired guards to do the stealing for them. And on top of this, those kites that survived were often found dead, poisoned by scavenging on baited carcasses put down for foxes and crows. As a result and despite various efforts by well-wishers the population of red kites in Wales by the 1970s had shrunk to below 24 pairs.

So this was the background against which the team, in May 1990, were making their film. Some of them were also involved in a major project for the release in this country of red kite chicks brought in from abroad and will have been aware of the part a successful film would play in winning public support. After careful planning two suitable sites were identified, one in the Chilterns, using chicks from Spain and the other near Inverness using chicks from Sweden. Both projects proved sufficiently successful to encourage follow-up programmes in other carefully chosen locations across the country and in this way colonies were established which were soon large enough for birds to link up with each other by natural dispersal. And so it was that in 1995 four red kites were recorded here in Sussex - the first in the county for 200 years - and tagging revealing that they came here from the Chiltern colony. In the ensuing 20 years numbers have increased steadily so that breeding populations are now well-established along the Downs and adjacent woodland, so that we can now once again enjoy the sight of these elegant birds without trekking off to Wales, a triumph for conservation.

Writing these notes takes my mind back 40 years to when we were staying in a tiny Logis tucked away in the mountains of Central France. We had driven along a small isolated road and found a gently sloping hillside bathed in early summer sun. We had got out of the car to the smell of wild thyme and mint and had spent the morning amongst wild orchids and other flowers - we had found pretty butterflies with pretty names to match; Pearly Heath, Chequered Skipper and Shepherd's Fritillary were just three. And we had eaten our picnic watched by a large emerald-green praying mantis. Then, as we packed up, there came from across the valley a pair of red kites, the first I'd ever seen, their chestnut red bodies and wings splashed with creamy-white patches clear in the sunlight; their long forked tails quivering to adjust to the breeze. They swooped and soared and circled one another - after all, it was spring and love was in the air.

July 2015

Butterflies may be coping better than we think

If we were to believe everything we see and hear we could be excused if we thought that butterflies were on their last legs, but in all aspects except one they are actually looking after themselves quite well. The exception is, of course, the unhelpful way in which we humans manage the land in which they live. After all, fossil-remains embedded in amber 100 million years ago tell us that they have been around for quite some time. Evolution is the continuous process of adapting to changes in the surrounding environment, so if butterflies have managed to survive through the aeons of change thus far it is reasonable to expect that they can continue to do so.

The thing that distinguishes butterflies (and moths) from other insects is that they pass through a four-stage life cycle during each of which they are confronted by very different hazards. If, for example, as adults they encounter cold, wet weather they will have difficulty in flying, mating and laying eggs. Likewise a caterpillar hatching from an egg will die unless there is an immediate supply of exactly the right food-plant and this in turn depends upon rainfall and temperature. And finally as either an egg or pupa, the stages in which many hibernate, a mild damp winter favours those parasites which lie in wait and spell death. And finally because the needs of each species are different what might seem to be an advantage for one may be a problem for another.

So climate is an important element at any of four stages in a butterfly's life and there is no doubt that abrupt changes in normal weather patterns can hit hard. But numbers always seem to build up again. Our much-loved small tortoiseshells provide an excellent example. These butterflies lay eggs in clusters on nettles and are heavily parasitized by flies which inject eggs directly into the bodies of their caterpillars. As a consequence numbers have always fluctuated, but re-built quickly – that is to say until about eight years ago when a new fly arrived from the continent which attacked the pupae, and just to make matters worse this new hazard was followed by two long hot summers which reduced the availability of the fresh young nitrogen-rich nettles sought out by egg-laying females. As a consequence numbers crashed and for several years small tortoiseshells were invisible. Last year, however, there was a tentative recovery and this year numbers are back to normal again. In fact as I write I can see no less than five newly hatched feeding on the thyme just under the window.

The main evolutionary device for ensuring survival is, of course, adaptation by physical change. But this process is slow, depending as it does on a chance genetic mutation that produces an advantage in the battle to survive which then spreads through the population. Nevertheless it is a continuous process across all life-forms and there are clear examples around for us to see. For instance when parts of the midlands countryside was affected by industrial pollution several species of butterfly and moth developed darker variants which were better camouflaged than the norm and therefore became dominant. But when the pollution was reversed the norm once again became dominant and the darker variant died out. This phenomenon is known as industrial melanism and very much the same thing happens amongst some very weak-flying butterflies where those living their entire lives in the shady side of a field have become darker than those of the same species in the same field but living in parts bathed in bright sunshine. Here again the beneficial gene provides better camouflage.

A recent announcement from the Met Office tells us that by the year 2100 an average summer day will be as hot as the extremes reached during the first week of this year's Wimbledon, and that winters by then will invariably be wet and mild. Trends in this direction have already had an impact upon the distribution of some butterflies, bringing about a drift northwards. A spectacular example was the arrival in West Sussex of several continental swallowtails in the late summer of 2013. Eggs were laid, caterpillars hatched and before winter set in fourteen pupae had entered hibernation and were kept under close observation; would they or would they not survive a typical English winter? In the event the winter was too mild to provide a conclusive test and they did survive to hatch in the spring of 2014 – one near Chichester where the event was greeted with great excitement by presenters from *Springwatch* who included the episode on tele. The hope was that the hatching butterflies would meet up or be reinforced by new immigrants with whom they could mate and establish a resident population here. But it seems that there were too few around and this happy event must be for another day.

Finally news about honey-buzzards, mis-named as they are, being neither buzzards nor feeders upon honey. But they do look sufficiently like common buzzards often to be mistaken, and they do raid the nests of social bees and wasps to feed on the larvae and adults, thick, greasy feathers and heavy scales on large, strong talons protecting them from stings. A few come here each year late in spring to nest and then return to Scandinavia. Their secretive habits and similarity to common buzzards may well lead to their numbers being under-reported and last week *The Times* carried news of the arrival in south-east England of what they described as "unusual numbers". By coincidence that same day we found in our garden a wasp's nest built in the ground amongst long grass. which had been trampled flat as if by a visiting dog. The nest itself had been scratched out and pulled apart, the scene matching in every detail the description in my book of the work of a honey-buzzard. I never saw the bird, but what else could it have been?

August 2015.

Nature Matters

Summer drifts into autumn

Those of us who do what Beth tells us to will be rewarded with gardens that remain fresh and colourful all year round, even in the dreary days of mid-winter. But in the wider countryside things are very different. There, life in all its forms is left to its own devices and now, as the bright greens of high-summer turn into the browns of old age, there is a lack of freshness and debris builds up. Gardeners sweep this up and make compost but in the wild it stays where it falls and rots, thereby setting in motion the vital processes of regeneration. Inevitably therefore autumn is a time when the countryside appears to be in decline, an impression reinforced by many of the butterflies that hatched earlier and, having achieved their mission to secure the next generation, have long since lost the beauty of youth. Now all they want is peace and quiet.

Red Admiral

Meanwhile other butterflies are busy building themselves up for the long winter sleep that is hibernation, and this is a time for us to check out the old wives' tale that red admirals only sip the fermented juice from rotting apples to get mildly intoxicated. There is, though, more to them than just that. Older books, for instance, tell us that the UK population is composed entirely of immigrants from the continent and that it is their off-spring that congregate in southern England in late summer as if intending to emigrate back across the Channel. But no reverse emigration actually occurs, nor did red admirals (in the past) hibernate. So it was rightly concluded that, come the cold weather, they simply died. But recently things have changed, our milder winters often enabling many to enter into a state of semi-hibernation from which they emerge to fly around whenever the sun shines, mating and laying eggs as conditions allow. When spring comes they are joined by a fresh wave of immigrants and as a consequence red admirals may nowadays pop up here at any time, all the year round. But things are different for their near-relatives, the small tortoiseshells. These are the ones that come into our houses in the autumn, intending to settle down for an uninterrupted six-month snooze. For them, though, this strategy has potentially fatal consequences if, later, indoor heating warms them up and they start to fly around using up irreplaceable reserves of food. Friends seeing this happen in their own houses often ring to ask what they should do and the answer is to wait for the butterfly to settle and then lift it by its folded wings and put it somewhere else much cooler but preferably still under cover.

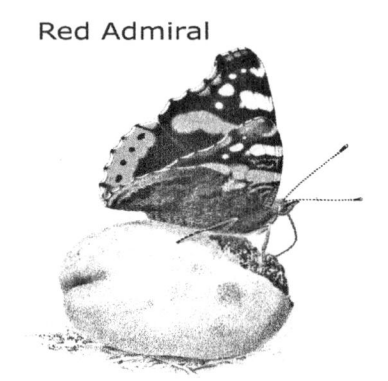

For butterfly enthusiasts late summer has one last treat; the delicately marked brown hairstreak which hatches in mid-August and is still flying at its pristine best well into September. There is only one problem - they are very hard to find. This is partly because they are rare and partly because they spend most of their time high up in the canopy of ash trees and are only seen when the females descend briefly, usually between 10am and 4pm, to lay their eggs on the fresh twigs of blackthorn. Despite this, or maybe because of it, brown hairstreaks have acquired a cult following, people gathering at known locations each year as summer ends. They come with binoculars, cameras, and sometimes with picnics and over the years a camaraderie has built up such that even if sightings have been few, the outings are adjudged a success. Passers-by seeing such gatherings may be tempted to giggle but the greater truth, surely, has more to do with the simple pleasure that comes with spending time in the company of wild nature.

Birds, too, contribute to the unique ambience of autumn. Family duties are over, likewise song, and all is silent. Apart from Susan Kitchener's nest box which was still in use by house sparrows in August and wood pigeons that are performing their courting routines on the telephone wire running up Sandy Lane even as we go to press, that's about it. The rooks that nested in colonies around the village have long since dispersed, some going as far as the continent, and when they return their numbers will swell as others from Russia and eastern Europe join them. By mid-September they will have formed flocks of several hundred, birds moving noisily between day-time feeding grounds and overnight roosts: a sure sign that winter is approaching. Others such as robins hide out of sight after raising their families to moult. This is not, as some say, because they do not wish be seen when looking so bedraggled but rather that their moult includes the shedding of flight feathers and is therefore a time of great peril. So they are sensibly hiding from predators.

Most bird movement at this time of year is part and parcel of the bi-annual migration and is sometimes surprisingly spread out over time. For example ospreys that had been nesting up north were already drifting southward through Sussex on their way back to Africa before the end of June. So too male black-tailed godwits still in their rich chestnut breeding plumage that were feeding at Pagham Harbour as early as mid-July – having apparently left their partners behind in Iceland to get on with raising their families. This dereliction of paternal duty is excelled by an elegant little wader called the curlew-sandpiper which passes through here on its way between Australia and the melting ice-floes of the Russian Arctic where it nests. So unappealing do the males find this choice of breeding ground that they stay on site no more than a couple of weeks; just long enough to ensure that the eggs their ladies lay bear fruit.

September 2015

The fascination of nature

When recently President Obama invited Sir David Attenborough to the White House for a televised chat, the host got things going by asking his guest what it was that first sparked his interest in wildlife. Sir David replied that it was hard to say because he really could not remember a time when it wasn't so; what's more, he said, it's been the same with every small child he has ever met. Kenneth Grahame must have recognised the truth of this when, over a century ago, he wrote Wind in the Willows. And the same with Beatrix Potter; how many of today's naturalists, I wonder, had their first encounter as a child with animals in the pages of her books. Brought up in the Victorian tradition few since have been able to match her skills as both a story-teller and picture-maker and her influence upon her young readers was both profound and enduring.

Those of us whose formative years came before, say, the 1950's were able to nourish our interests in nature by being collectors. Anything would do. My own collection stretched to feathers, bones of small mammals extracted from regurgitated owls pellets and glued to cardboard and even, for a brief period, a grass snake - brief because when I took it to school in a box a po-faced master confiscated it and, when he thought I wasn't looking, let it go. But birds' eggs and butterflies were the main thing. I used to breed through the caterpillars of butterflies and moths in cages bought with my pocket money from a dealer in Kent. I was egged on by an older brother and a near-neighbour, a retired doctor and keen lepidopterist who had an apple orchard where Eyed Hawk-moths laid eggs and the caterpillars fed on the leaves. We also had apple trees but my father sprayed them so there were no caterpillars. This is why my brother and I visited the doctor, bagging the branches to contain the caterpillars and when they had pupated we each took a couple home, nurturing them through the winter and then in spring when they hatched add them to our collection. And so now, 77 years on, Eyed Hawk- moths have a very special place in my affections.

Later on the killing of live things for the purpose of collecting fell out of fashion and soon in many cases became illegal. But for butterfly enthusiasts in particular there was salvation in the form of the huge advances made in the design of cameras, so that before long even amateurs were able to take photographs in close-up that captured and preserved for ever the beauty of, say, a butterfly delicately posed on a wild flower, proboscis extended and sipping nectar. Such a picture endures for ever and tells a story a hundred times more evocative than a cabinet full of faded insects secured by a pin. Today's successors to yesterday's collectors are most likely those whose enthusiasm now directs them towards such work as the manual preservation and restoration of habitat, walking transects and keeping records; all vital to the cause of conservation.

Nature Matters

There are so many ways in which wildlife works its fascinations; the social lives of termites, for instance, or the migration of elvers from their birthplace far upstream in European rivers to the Sargasso Sea in the Caribbean where they grow to become adult eels, then make the return journey of several thousand miles back to their natal rivers to spawn. Or the ingenuity with which a spider spins its web, seen at its best still wet with dew and back-lit by early-morning sun. Yet one that is around us all the time and is therefore easily overlooked is the sheer physical beauty of it all. So an occasional jolt to remind us to look again can be helpful and this is exactly what is provided by a just-published book of flower paintings by Rory McEwen called *The Colours of Reality*. Born in 1932 in Ayrshire, educated at Eton and Cambridge, McEwen drove a purple Ferrari and was a frequent guest at shooting parties at Balmoral, an unlikely background for one who was to become a success in the pop music scene of the early 1950s. Yet this is what happened, his singing voice and mastery of the 12-string guitar quickly winning fame on both sides of the Atlantic. However his abiding interest lay in painting flowers and this was to become his life's work. Using hand-prepared vellum and brushes cut to the finest points, he developed a style based on the gradual building up of paint in a way that reflected light and shade: all in a detail that demanded the wearing of a watch-makers eye-glass. In 1982, aged just 50 McEwen died of brain cancer and two years ago an exhibition of his paintings was held at Kew. Now a selection has been reproduced in this book and for anyone who might wish to be reminded of the exquisite beauty of nature's simplest things, time spent with these paintings will be rewarding.

A story that tells how wildlife can restore our faith in times of stress comes from Major-General Christopher Lipscombe who, in June 1944, lead the 4th Battalion of the Somerset Light Infantry in their landing on the beaches of Arromanches. In the course of leading his men across Europe to the gates of Belsen he won the DSO and bar and throughout the traumas of battle found solace in recording all the butterflies he saw along the way. Just two instances give us a flavour. Whilst taking cover in a slit trench and under heavy fire he recalls being uplifted by a Black Hairstreak joining him to drink from the newly-dug earth beside him. And another time he tells of his joy, when exploring terrain from which the enemy had just been driven, of finding a large colony of Chalkhill Blues in which 20% of the females were a rare aberrant form *syngrapha*. "A most homely diversion and a great comfort" he later wrote.

October 2015

Nature Matters

Some good places for birds

Each year between late September and early November several million birds come to this country for the winter and because some are the same species as those that live here all year round it can be difficult to pick them out. Blackbirds, chaffinches and several of the tit family are just a few examples. Amongst those that look very different are the geese that fly in from as far away as Greenland and Arctic Russia. These journeys are so arduous that they fly in tight V-shaped formations made up of family groups. This way the birds create air currents that aid those behind and old hands who know the way take it in turns in front. Little wonder that the same birds arrive in exactly the same place each winter.

Once geese have settled into their winter quarters and the daily routine has become little more than shuttling between on-shore feeding grounds and off-shore night-time roosts the V-formation is abandoned in favour of small, untidy and very noisy flocks. The two geese species we see around here, graylag and Canada, live permanently in this country but both are descended from migratory forebears. The first Canada geese to come here were brought in from North America by King Charles II to adorn his collection of exotics on the lake in St James's Park in London. As a consequence a fashion was set and soon Canada geese became regulars on the lakes of stately homes across the country, soon to escape into the wild and become a part of our native avifauna. With graylags the story is slightly different. In many places they are migratory, but in England they are resident, having descended from domestic birds, that were farmed for food and the supply of wing-feathers to the makers of quill pens. The only migrant graylags coming here for the winter are from Iceland and remain in Scotland.

A sense of the magic that huge flocks of geese can bring to the winter coastal scene will be available to us on television early in November when BBC's Autumn Watch visits Caerlaverock on the Solway Firth to film the barnacle geese from Svalbard. Down here the only migratory geese that visit us in any numbers are the much smaller dark-bellied form of brents. They come here having nested on the Taimyr Peninsula in Arctic Russia and bring with them a glamour that often accompanies visitors from far-off and remote places. Large flocks graze in the meadows behind Pagham Harbour and there is an infectious excitement when late in the day they rise in large flocks to spend the night out on the safety of the water. There is much else to see thereabouts but this alone makes a journey down to Pagham worthwhile, Along the Arun valley, stretching from the Wiggonholt RSPB Reserve, south to Waltham Marsh and across Amberley water-meadows to the Downs, lies one of the most prolific areas for wildlife in the south of England. Winter bird staples are wigeon, pintail, teal, shoveller and gadwell but it is worth keeping an eye on the Sussex Ornithological Society web-site (www.sos/sightings) to see what else is about. And it isn't just birds that are special; the adjacent water meadows, particularly around Amberley, are considered the richest in the country for wetland flora and dragonflies.

There are also attractions for birders up on the Downs. A good place can be reached by taking the lane east out of North Stoke, manageable by car as far as a locked gate at TQ039111. From there bear right on foot along a track for about ½ a mile to a spot noted on the map as The Burgh (TQ045111). These precise instructions should enable anyone interested to find a place where food is put out for grey partridges and this acts as a magnet for ground-vermin and other birds. Both corn and reed buntings and yellowhammers are regulars and these in turn attract raptor such as red kites, common buzzards and short-eared owls. The occasional hen harrier and merlin have also been seen. And just to round things off, ravens have recently established a winter roost nearby.

Over the Downs and on along the Arun there is the joy of the Wildfowl and Wetland Trust Reserve at Arundel which, in addition to the display enclosures containing captive exotics, offers fine views over wetlands that are unobtrusively but effectively managed for wild birds. Hides are provided from which these can be seen in comfort and often at close range, going about their every-day lives unstressed by the proximity of humans. And then on to the coast itself. There are several good spots to choose from but anywhere from Pagham Harbour going west to Chichester Harbour is unlikely to be a disappointment, especially as recent coastal re-construction has provided an opportunity to create a new bird-friendly area called Medmerry Reserve. This links Pagham and Church Norton with the coast west of Selsey Bill. For the time being a visit to Medmerry involves a long walk from the car-park at Earnley to the beach. But there are rewards for those who persevere. For instance in the spring of 2014 the first black-winged stilts to nest in Britain for 27 years came to Medmerry to join their near-relatives, the avocets already established there. Each of these birds has a distinctive gracefulness of its own and to have them at the same time side by side is very special.

November 2015

Nature Matters

Shades of white – 5 birds and a moth

Most stories about wildlife these days tell us that this or that animal or plant is on the verge of being wiped out and, furthermore, that this is usually the result of careless human activity. For this reason it is right and proper that we should be told. But there is the risk that, through reporting bias, we never hear the good news. So here are five stories about birds that are doing increasingly well which may redress the balance. In the right season all can now be found along the Arun valley and adjacent stretches of coast; all are mostly white, easy to see and identify and above all radiate a persona such that if they were plants nurserymen would call them "architectural".

First avocets, handsome birds, white except for a black head and wing fringes but best known for their long beaks that, towards their ends, tilt upwards. This makes it an ideal tool for wading in shallow water and scooping up food on the surface with side-to-side sweeps but not so good when conditions are different. For this reason two centuries ago their stronghold in Britain were the fens of East Anglia where there were wide expanses of shallow water. But this, too, brought problems; such concentrations made them easy prey to the habits of the times, namely that if a bird looked that good it risked ending up either on a dinner plate or stuffed in a glass case. Added to this their eggs were ruthlessly harvested for food, and so when the fens were drained that was it; 1842 was the last time avocets nested in Britain.

But then in 1947 came a miracle; throughout the 2nd World War much of the coast of East Anglia had been closed to the public. So when a stray shell fired from a nearby range damaged a sluice along the coast of Suffolk and several pairs of avocets were found nesting there the excitement was extreme. Fortunately there were birders on hand able to see that the non-maintenance of coastal defences during the war had allowed conditions to return to exactly the state required by these specialised feeders and thus began an exercise in habitat management which was to result in the gradual spread of these elegant birds all the way from Norfolk down and along the south coast and on up to the Mersey. Today a special treat is to visit the hides that overlook the lagoon on Brownsea Island where winter flocks exceeding 1,000 avocets feed in the shallows behind the sea wall.

Another magnificent wader with feeding habits similar to avocets except that it uses a huge spatulate bill to sift the water is aptly named the spoonbill. These birds once bred extensively in the UK but in common with populations elsewhere, numbers have suffered from drainage, fishing and water-related recreation. The last time a spoonbill bred in this country was late in the

Spoonbill

17th century and one reason for its demise is suggested by glancing at the menu set before Cardinal Wolseley to mark his visit to Kings Lynn in 1522; succulent young spoonbills were the centre-piece of a table that bore also 3 bitterns, 10 cygnets, 12 capons, 13 plovers, 8 pike and 3 tench. But happily incontinence even on this grand scale did not prevent long-term survival and, as so often with water birds, the Dutch polders provided the necessary sanctuary. Numbers there have grown extensively and the overflow has pushed birds back across into East Anglia. From there they have spread out and, although breeding spoonbills remain a rarity in the UK sightings of non-breeders are increasing and can occur at any time of year. Indeed, from time to time a stray spoonbill drops in just down the road at Pulborough Marshes.

Finally the three egrets; little, great white and cattle. Birders visiting wetlands in Europe will be familiar with all three. In the breeding season little egrets have long frilly plumes growing from their crests, backs and chests which were once prized worldwide by ladies of fashion. For instance in India in 1914 one oz of feathers was selling at 28 times the price of the same weight in silver and the resulting carnage is put at 200 million birds annually. Never more than a vagrant in this country, the first little egrets to breed here did so in Poole Harbour just 20 years ago. Since then they have spread rapidly around our coasts and inland along rivers, relishing, it seems, our more benign climate of recent years. Things are now such that seeing half a dozen feeding in the rain-sodden field just below our bedroom window here in Sandy Lane last winter was no more than a mild surprise. Cattle egrets and great white egrets are less frequent but also increasing.

Now to the moth - more precisely the ghost moth. In mid-summer the whitest of white males, assemble as if they were tiny capercaillie about to perform their annual lek. Michael Blencowe, Vice-Chairman of Sussex Butterfly Conservation witnessed this event last June and has kindly allowed me to relate his story;

"In the dimming twilight a white moth rose from the grass and hung in the air – a ghost moth. Soon dozens of them were all swaying around me. Some remained in their stations while others swung erratically and crashed into their neighbours. The daylight was fading quickly and soon all that was left was the seemingly luminous white wings of the waltzing ghost moths. The whole silent scene felt otherworldly – as if I had stumbled into a ceremony performed by miniature white-robed druids. As the moonlight illuminated the glade the action slowed and the moths dispersed. I almost felt like applauding."

Entertaining as this was, Michael reminds us that the moth's whiteness serves the same purpose as the flashy white suit worn by John Travolta in *Saturday Night Fever*; the most flamboyant males attracting the pick of the ladies.

December 2015

The earthworm's salvation

Born 19 years ago, Dolly the sheep was the first animal to be reproduced by cloning. There was general outrage and things didn't turn out well. More recently came Winnie, a dachshund so much loved by his owner, a lady in England, that she entered him into a competition run by genetic engineers in South Korea. First prize was a free cloning. Winnie won and so came into being Winnie-mini and the blood-line was secured. On the open market this cloning would have cost £60,000 but since then prices appear to have plummeted to the point where China now say that they plan to produce a million cattle a year by cloning. Consider this in the context of robots capable of doing the heavy lifting and the demonstrable ability of ladies to do many jobs just as well as the men who used to do them and we men begin to wonder what is to become of us.

For guidance let us look elsewhere in the animal kingdom. The perfect model for traditional family life is provided by kestrels. These birds forego building a nest, so the first serious work is to lay and incubate eggs. The female attends to both these tasks and is fed at the nest throughout by the male. This division of labour continues until the eggs have hatched and the young have flown. Only then does the female resume the chore of hunting for herself and the male gets free time to recuperate. Phalaropes, on the other hand, prefer a more modern arrangement; the females take the dominant role in pair-selection and mating, so have the jollier plumage. Thereafter all they do is deposit eggs in any convenient hollow in the ground and then push off, leaving the males to incubate the eggs and raise the chicks unaided. Other bird species divide the tasks variously, some pairing for life and others setting new extremes in promiscuity.

Let us now pass over the different spiders wherein the female concludes the nuptial proceedings by eating her mate and proceed directly to earthworms. These animals are hermaphrodite which means that each individual worm creates both eggs and the cells necessary to fertilize them. Pairing is still required, however, because self-fertilisation dangerously weakens the gene-pool. But the ceremony is brief, simple and, beyond occurring on a warm spring evening, without romance. Two neighbouring but unacquainted worms, peep out above ground, come together so that each can simultaneously fertilize the other's eggs and then retire. Their job done, they have no further contact. The eggs are expelled from the body in a cacoon and left to hatch. But remember; if all animals dumbed things down to the same extent there would be other far-reaching consequences. Just for starters, birds, freed from the need for elaborate courtship, would not sing nor require ornate plumage. Nor would the males of the many species that fight each other over mates require things like fangs and horns, thereby denying the presenters of

Autumn Watch the opportunity of commenting on scenes of rutting stags in tones of mounting excitement more appropriate to the Grand National.

Back to earthworms; some 800 million years ago worm-like creatures were amongst the first to creep from the sea onto muddy land. Some stayed above ground and evolved into many different species of which we humans are one. Others wriggled under the mud and stayed there, evolving with fairly modest changes into the earthworms we know today. Their bodies are simple segmented tubes held in shape by muscles and a sort of all-purpose internal fluid. They live in underground tunnels and move by bunching themselves up and then thrusting their front-ends forward. They gain traction from minute bristles on the surface of their skin, the efficiency of which may be judged by watching a bird struggling to pull a worm from its burrow.

All segments are anatomically the same except for the fifth which encloses the organs of reproduction and the first wherein the nerves that coordinate simple reflexes come together. This is the nearest that worms come to having a brain. Moles can nip it off thereby disorienting the hapless victim without killing it. They then store it, immobilised, in a larder thus ensuring an ample supply of fresh food. Workers have found larders stacked with a dozen or so earthworms awaiting their grizzly fate. However a problem lurks; unless eaten within five days the head will re-generate, enabling the earthworm to wriggle free. So more experienced moles further incommode their catch by tying them into a knot. All this can only lead to the conclusion that earthworms have a pretty miserable life, lived out in an extremely unlovely place under-ground. So perhaps their salvation - remember they have survived with little change for 800 million years - lies in the fact that they don't really have a brain at all; certainly not one that enables them to realise how miserable they should feel. Ignorance is, in their case, bliss.

In a way this is a pity because earthworms actually perform an important function without realising it. They do this by dragging leaves from the surface down into their tunnels and mixing them with soil. Then, using the peristalsis of their muscles, they pass the mix through their bodies, ejecting the void from their back-ends either into the tunnel or upwards where it appears above ground as a worm-casting. And this is where it becomes so important; the whole process both aerates and adds nutrients to the soil. We can get a measure of the scale of it all from the fact that in a typical English meadow the combined body-weight of all the earthworms slaving away just inches below ground-level exceeds that of all the cattle grazing above, and for this reason worms deserve much of the credit for the lush forests and vegetation that is vital to the welfare of our planet.

Is this, then, a task to which we redundant men of the future can look forward?
January 2016

Now and then

Born in 1720, Gilbert White spent his childhood exploring the countryside around the family home at Selborne in Hampshire and developed a love of nature that remained with him for the rest of his life. His grandfather had been the parish priest and it was the young Gilbert's ambition to follow in his footsteps and to be able to combine his ministry with the further study of the surrounding wildlife. But his plans were thwarted when, upon his ordination, he discovered that the living in Selborne was in the gift of Magdalen College, Oxford so that he, a graduate of Oriel, could not be considered. But his determination endured and when the lesser post of curate at Selborne fell vacant he, by then aged 51, unmarried and of independent means, took it with glee. And it is easy to see why; a countryside in which to roam as beautiful as a Constable painting and wildlife more varied and more plentiful than anything we know to-day all beckoned. Gilbert White will have been without many of today's creature-comforts but even so there will have been much for a naturalist of today to envy. He was to live another 22 years, time enough for his exceptional powers of observation and record-keeping to put him at the forefront of amateur naturalists.

These were times when the study of the natural world was mostly in the domain of scientists whose work was confined to the laboratory. White however was the opposite; his observations came entirely from the field and as a consequence he is often spoken of as the father of ecology. His work was and still is so highly regarded that his best-known book, *The Natural History and Antiquities of Selborne* first published in 1788, has never since been out of print. There are many solid achievements to his name. He was, for example, the first to identify that the three warblers, chiffchaff, willow warbler and wood warbler, previously thought to be the same birds, were in fact three separate species. He was also the first to identify noctule bats and harvest mice, so it is easy to forgive him for arguing that swallows did not leave this country in winter, believing instead that they hid in holes in the ground during the worst of the weather, coming out to fly around whenever it was warm enough. Nor was he the only one to be bamboozled by bird migration - a famous misconception of the day concerned the barnacle geese that come here each winter from their breeding grounds in the high Arctic. There were many who believed that these birds spent the summer round our shores in the form of the barnacles we find in our rock-pools. Hence the name.

In addition to his field-notes Gilbert White's writings provide some interesting insights into the prevailing norms of the day. For instance, although many people had a sensitive regard for the countryside and its wildlife, there was none of today's intense pressure to conserve what remains before it disappears. Furthermore life for many was harsh and if a little extra could be earned on the side from, say, poaching or robbing a bird's nest and selling of eggs to a collector, what's the harm? There was plenty more where that came from. Interestingly *The Natural History and Antiquities of Selborne* includes a letter from Gilbert White to a friend written on 7th May 1779 which tells of *"three brace of birds* (note the language of the field-sportsman) *too uncommon to have obtained an English name"* and goes on to give the Latin name and an accurate description of what turned out to be black-winged stilts, six of which had turned up at Frensham Pond near Farnham where, the letter says, the pond-keeper shot five and *"having satisfied his curiosity* (i.e shot them) *did spare the sixth"*. Today we would condemn this as an act of flagrant vandalism, the more so as the pond-keeper did this to sell the skins to a taxidermist. Worse still, White seems to have regarded all this with so little concern that he himself ended up with one of the birds mounted in a glass case for his own collection.

To-day black-winged stilts in this country are at best rare vagrants with just two records of successful breeding, one in Nottinghamshire in 1945 and one in Norfolk in 1987. On the few occasions that I have seen them it has always been in wetlands of rare beauty tucked away out of sight around the Mediterranean where bird and place come together in perfect harmony. So imagine the excitement amongst local birders when in May 2014 a pair were seen preparing to nest amongst workers engaged in restoring coastal defences at what is now an RSPB reserve at Medmerry just west of Selsey. Immediate steps were taken to ensure their safety and when 3 eggs appeared in simple scrape amongst the pebbles a 24-hour watch was arranged, volunteers from the Sussex Ornithological Society taking the daylight shifts and others from a professional security company watching at night. Work on coastal reconstruction was re-arranged to minimise interference and a workman's hut was given over for use by the guards. Soon after they hatched, the chicks were led by their parents out onto the mud-flats where observation was difficult and their continued survival could only be presumed from noisy parental activity. But soon the guards felt it safe to approach by foot and found the chicks nearly fledged, and a few days later the family decamped a few miles to Pagham Harbour's Ferry Pool, a famous hot-spot for water-birds. Then, believe it or not, they flew north over the Downs to Wiggonholt where they spent two days before returning briefly to Ferry Pool. Then finally, on 11th August, the whole family took wing southward to join up with others far to the south. Magic

But what, I wonder, would Gilbert White have made of such a palaver!

February 2016

Survival by adaptation

Although the impact of changing climate is often in the news no mention is ever made of the fact that the environment on our planet has been in a state of constant flux from the beginning of time. To ignore this is to miss the fact that our present-day fauna and flora is the outcome of several hundred millions years of adaptation to change and therefore has some experience in the art of survival. Life adapts for three reasons; first to equip itself to exploit new habitats, second to obtain a competitive advantage over others, and third to remain viable on a planet that has always been, and still is, in a state of change. Fossil remains tell us much about ancestral life-forms and have long fascinated naturalists but the topic of adaptation only entered the mainstream of science in 1858 when Charles Darwin and Alfred Wallace presented a joint paper to the Linnaean Society in London. Their proposition was that all animals, including those from the same species, have individual, perhaps even unique, variations in their make-up which will be passed on to subsequent generations and if by chance there are any which enhance survival, then a process of natural selection ensures that those so blessed will eventually dominate, and conversely those without it will perish. This process, they argued, lies at the heart of evolution.

Both Darwin and Wallace had reached this conclusion independently based on studies of their vast collections, in Wallace's case mostly of insects from the East Indies and in Darwin's from various specimens of finches collected from different islands that make up the Galapagos. But neither knew the mechanics by which such characteristics were passed from generation to generation and as a consequence the assembled scientists, already uncomfortable with the underlying suggestion that mankind may have descended from the same ancestors as lower forms of life, rejected the thesis. However soon afterwards a Czech geneticist called Gregor Mendel was to publish work which demonstrated that material which he called genes are present in all animals. These genes, carried by both male and female, are imprinted with the characteristics that are inheritable and come together when new life is created. This ensures both the integrity of the species concerned and the inheritance of the variations that drive evolution. Mendel's discovery in conjunction with the work of Darwin and Wallace made a compelling case for the theory of evolution and set the scene for further research. As a consequence we can today attribute all aspects of any animal, be it its physiology or its behaviour, to the constant battle for competitive advantage and survival. And this process goes on all around us, even today.

So the question is, will all this be sufficient to enable wildlife to survive present-day climate change? Well much depends upon the rate of reproduction and there will be winners and losers. An example of the latter occurred some 65.5 million years ago when a meteor hit Earth and triggered a sharp drop in temperature that dinosaurs, the dominant animals of the time, were unable to survive. The reason is thought to be that it became too cold for their eggs which they left untended in the open, to hatch. If true, this cleared the way for mammals which retain their embryos within the warmth of their bodies to assume dominance. This event was so sudden that it left no time to adapt and it probably wiped out other animals as well. In this context one thinks of today's polar bears; they are trapped within a rapidly shrinking habitat upon which they are totally dependent and it is difficult to think of any genetic modification which could help them. But even were there one – and remember variations occur at random, not by design – they are slow breeders and therefore their ability to adapt at the required speed is unlikely. By comparison a rabbit, born in the spring, is a parent by autumn, producing litters of up to 10 young several times a year, a rate of reproduction which enables them to produce mutant genes that spread through the population rapidly, making them good survivors. Or a mosquito which can complete its 4-stage life-cycle in just 2 weeks, each female laying many eggs. Mutant genes spread rapidly, a measure of their success being that there are 3,500 species world-wide.

Another survival device used especially by birds is re-location. The trigger is usually a shortage of food so the best survivors are those that are the most versatile feeders. Starlings, by preference insect eaters, have addressed this problem by adapting their beaks and muscles to probe the ground and open up holes. This has increased their menu to include other things like worms, so broadening their distribution. Robins are another example; since the advent of bird tables these ground-feeders have taken to eating from nut-feeders. To begin with they jumped up flapping their wings, using up more energy than their thin pickings replaced. But now they are able to hold on with their feet and use their beaks as efficiently as tits. Whether this has required bodily adaptation which will be passed on to their offspring or was achieved by imitating tits I do not know but either way it illustrates that small adaptations are happening all the time.

And another that can only be the result of innate skill and not a little intelligence comes from the out-back of Australia where the story goes that black kites have taken to scavenging around picnic areas, picking up bits of bread and dropping them over water. This lures fish to the surface which they pounce upon and eat. The story then goes on to say that these same birds have also learnt that the scales on their feet are sufficiently thick to enable them to pick up glowing embers from picnic fires. These they then place amongst nearby dry vegetation to start a new fire. This way they flush out frogs, lizards and small mice, all of which rate highly amongst a black kite's culinary delights…..The stories are endless, but I have reached the bottom of the page; so that must suffice for now!

March 2016

sharp drop in temperature that dinosaurs, the dominant animals of the time, were unable to survive. The reason is thought to be that it became too cold for their eggs which they left untended in the open, to hatch. If true, this cleared the way for mammals which retain their embryos within the warmth of their bodies to assume dominance. This event was so sudden that it left no time to adapt and it probably wiped out other animals as well. In this context one thinks of today's polar bears; they are trapped within a rapidly shrinking habitat upon which they are totally dependent and it is difficult to think of any genetic modification which could help them. But even were there one – and remember variations occur at random, not by design – they are slow breeders and therefore their ability to adapt at the required speed is unlikely. By comparison a rabbit, born in the spring, is a parent by autumn, producing litters of up to 10 young several times a year, a rate of reproduction which enables them to produce mutant genes that spread through the population rapidly, making them good survivors. Or a mosquito which can complete its 4-stage life-cycle in just 2 weeks, each female laying many eggs. Mutant genes spread rapidly, a measure of their success being that there are 3,500 species world-wide.

Another survival device used especially by birds is re-location. The trigger is usually a shortage of food so the best survivors are those that are the most versatile feeders. Starlings, by preference insect eaters, have addressed this problem by adapting their beaks and muscles to probe the ground and open up holes. This has increased their menu to include other things like worms, so broadening their distribution. Robins are another example; since the advent of bird tables these ground-feeders have taken to eating from nut-feeders. To begin with they jumped up flapping their wings, using up more energy than their thin pickings replaced. But now they are able to hold on with their feet and use their beaks as efficiently as tits. Whether this has required bodily adaptation which will be passed on to their offspring or was achieved by imitating tits I do not know but either way it illustrates that small adaptations are happening all the time.

And another that can only be the result of innate skill and not a little intelligence comes from the out-back of Australia where the story goes that black kites have taken to scavenging around picnic areas, picking up bits of bread and dropping them over water. This lures fish to the surface which they pounce upon and eat. The story then goes on to say that these same birds have also learnt that the scales on their feet are sufficiently thick to enable them to pick up glowing embers from picnic fires. These they then place amongst nearby dry vegetation to start a new fire. This way they flush out frogs, lizards and small mice, all of which rate highly amongst a black kite's culinary delights…..The stories are endless, but I have reached the bottom of the page; so that must suffice for now!

March 2016